THIS WEEKEND

A Seasonal Guide to Weekend Fun

LYNN GRISARD FULLMAN

CRANE HILL
PUBLISHERS

This book is dedicated to

My parents, Margaret and Lindsay Grisard, who gave me life;
My brother, Jim, who gave me laughter;
My husband, Milton, who gave me love;
My daughters, Christine and Cameron, who gave me joy;
My God, who gave me life eternal.

Published by
Crane Hill Publishers
3608 Clairmont Avenue
Birmingham, AL 35222; www.cranehill.com

Printed in the United States of America

Library of Congress Cataloging-in-Publication Data

Fullman, Lynn Grisard.
Alabama this weekend: a seasonal guide to weekend fun/Lynn Grisard Fullman.
p.   cm.
ISBN 1-57587-082-7 (alk. paper)
1. Alabama—Guidebooks. I. Title.
F324.3.F86   1998
917.6104'63—dc21   97–52647
                                                              CIP

10   9   8   7   6   5   4   3   2   1

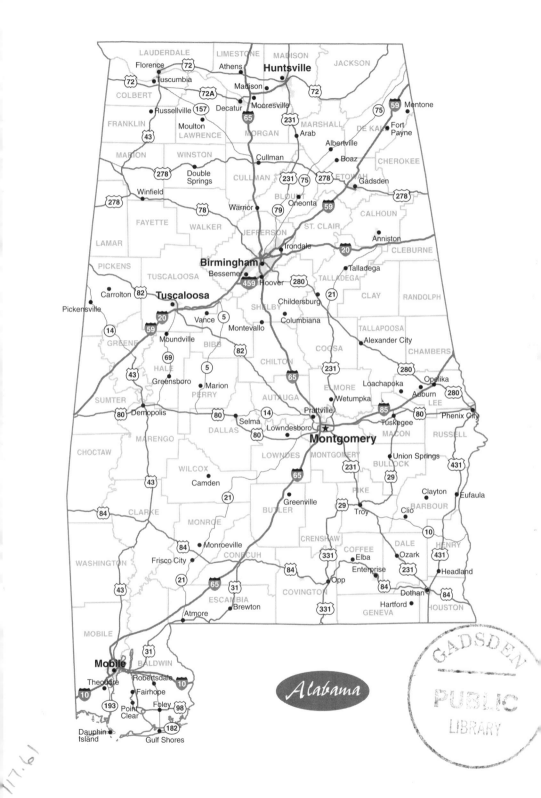

LAUDERDALE LIMESTONE MADISON JACKSON
Florence 72
72 Tuscumbia Athens Huntsville
72A 72
COLBERT Madison
Mooresville 75 59 Mentone
Russellville 157 Decatur 231 Fort
Moulton 65 MARSHALL DE KALB Payne
FRANKLIN 157 Arab Albertville
43 Moulton MORGAN
LAWRENCE
Winfield 278 Double Cullman Boaz CHEROKEE
MARION WINSTON Springs 231 75 278 Gadsden
278 CULLMAN 278
FAYETTE 78 Warrior BLOUNT 59
LAMAR WALKER 79 Oneonta CALHOUN
278 Anniston
PICKENS JEFFERSON Irondale ST. CLAIR CLEBURNE
Birmingham 20
TUSCALOOSA Bessemer Talladega
Carrollton 82 459 Hoover 280 TALLADEGA
Pickensville Tuscaloosa CLAY RANDOLPH
14 20 Vance 5 Childersburg 21
59 Columbiana
Moundville SHELBY
GREENE 69 Montevallo TALLAPOOSA
HALE 5 CHILTON Alexander City CHAMBERS
43 82 COOSA 280
Greensboro Marion 65 231 Opelika
SUMTER PERRY AUTAUGA Loachapoka Auburn 280
80 80 ELMORE Wetumpka 85 LEE
Demopolis 14 Prattville 80 Phenix City
MARENGO 80 Selma Tuskegee RUSSELL
Lowndesboro MACON
CHOCTAW DALLAS Montgomery
WILCOX LOWNDES MONTGOMERY Union Springs 431
43 231 BULLOCK
Camden 29
21 PIKE Clayton Eufaula
Greenville 29 Clio BARBOUR
84 BUTLER Troy 10
CLARKE MONROE CRENSHAW DALE HENRY
Monroeville COFFEE Ozark 431
84 331 Elba 231 Headland
Frisco City CONECUH Enterprise
WASHINGTON 21 65 Opp 84 Dothan 84
43 31 COVINGTON Hartford HOUSTON
ESCAMBIA 331 GENEVA
Brewton
Atmore

MOBILE
31
Mobile BALDWIN
Theodore Robertsdale 10
10 Fairhope
193 Foley 98
Point Clear
Dauphin 182
Island Gulf Shores

Alabama

TABLE OF CONTENTS

Fall

Winter

Year-Round

ACKNOWLEDGMENTS

A book, by some clerical necessity, bears most often the name of a single writer. But that name is only a hint of the credit due.

I owe a great debt of gratitude, beginning with my teachers at Girls Preparatory School, who instilled the belief that women can do anything. And I owe my parents, who have encouraged me unconditionally.

I owe my family who cheered me on, traveled with me, and edited me.

There are others living and working in Alabama who were generous in sharing their time, their knowledge, and their insights. Thanks and gratitude to:

• Pat Bellew, who knows all there is to know about Blount County

• Colette Boehm, with the Alabama Gulf Coast Convention and Visitors Bureau, for her enthusiasm about her sunny backyard

• Lin Graham, who knows Dothan and hospitality

• Susann Hamlin, the miracle worker with the Colbert County Tourism and Convention Bureau, who knows and loves this northwest corner of Alabama

• Dilcy Hilley, who helps the magic continue in the Magic City

•Heather Roberts, formerly with the Auburn–Opelika Convention and Visitors Bureau

•Georgia Carter Turner, with the Alabama Mountain Lakes Tourist Association, who has been endlessly patient and always willing to go beyond the call of duty— and does

• Patty Tucker, with the DeKalb County Tourist Association, who always took the time and did so with a smile

• Debbie Wilson, with Florence–Lauderdale Tourism, who knows and shares this region rich in attractions

• Milton Fullman, whose camera has caught memorable corners of Alabama, and whose life has decorated my own

• Ami Simpson and Cameron Reeder, with the Alabama Bureau of Tourism and Travel, whose unflagging patience with my quest for insight and detail knew no bounds.

INTRODUCTION

I am not an Alabama native, but having lived here longer than in my Tennessee hometown, I feel that my adoption is legal and binding. The people in this state have made me feel that these foothills of the Appalachians are my home.

Growing up in Chattanooga I was not far from Birmingham, a city that must have piqued my interest when my age barely reached double digits. I recently discovered proof in my attic. There I found stashed among my life's mementos a Chattanooga newspaper from the 1960s, with the front-page story focusing on Birmingham and the city's racial conflict. I no longer remember why, as a youngster, I found reports of the city's events intriguing enough to save. But I did.

While I was still a kid my Chattanooga neighbors moved to Birmingham and invited me to visit during the summers. I remember those times with happiness. My mother would pack a sack lunch, drive me to the Chattanooga train depot, and send me on my way. It was during those visits, when I was maybe ten or so, that I first fell in love with Alabama.

I rode alone on the train, pressing my face into the window, trying to see all that I could as I raced from north to south. I remember reading "See Rock City" on barn roofs and seeing small towns and kudzu, pickup trucks and farmhouses.

Once I arrived in Birmingham, my transplanted friends, Edna and Paul Russom, who were like second parents, made me feel like a queen. I would spend warm days being entertained, visiting the zoo, playing miniature golf, and jumping on trampolines that could be rented by the hour or half hour.

It was during one of those summer visits that I rode up U.S. Highway 31 to Vestavia Hills and glanced into the valley to discover Samford University. To me the campus was a mirage, a tiny town with lights, look-alike buildings, roadways, and specks for cars. Several years later as high-school graduation loomed, I applied only to Samford University and never considered what I would do if not accepted.

In the fall of 1967 I packed my things, moved to the Samford campus, and started a new chapter in my life.

With the college as my base I began to explore Alabama. One of my best discoveries was the man who would become my life's mate, Milton, a Samford student when we met. We married young, while Milton was in the U.S. Navy, and while the war in Vietnam was raging. As he trudged through his navy years as a hospital corpsman, I finished my undergraduate degree, and then moved to Virginia to be with him. When he completed his military duty in 1974 we moved

HOW TO USE
ALABAMA THIS WEEKEND

Doubters have wondered aloud how I would find a year's worth of things to do in Alabama. Little did they know that my problem would be narrowing the options.

I have suggested trips for particular seasons (spring, summer, fall, winter), but most of the excursions can be enjoyed anytime. That's one good thing about Alabama's pleasant, year-round climate.

As you travel, treat the listings in this book as a guide. Map out trips that fit your schedule and interests. If you discover something on your own, more's the better.

While I have worked to ensure accuracy, it is best to phone ahead to confirm that festivals still are held and museums still are in operation. Life is, after all, an ever-changing kaleidoscope.

Alabama This Weekend offers specific suggestions and helpful hints designed for successful outings. Contact a local chamber of commerce or convention and visitors bureau for additional restaurant and lodging possibilities. Don't forget too the value of input from a friend or local resident.

Please note: There is no charge for an event or accommodation to be included in this guidebook. I have personally chosen the entries based on my years of living and my decade as a travel writer.

It would have been impossible to include each of the state's sites, but I welcome your input for new suggestions. You may contact me through the Crane Hill Publishers web site, www.cranehill.com.

So sit back, enjoy reading this book, and then take some trips to really get to know Alabama, a state brimming with surprises. If I've done my job even half well, you will understand what prompted the song "Stars Fell on Alabama."

THIS WEEKEND

the mountain's brow is located midway between Mentone and DeSoto State Park.

If you get a hankering for city life, you'll find plenty of fast-food and chain restaurants in nearby Fort Payne.

Back at the Dude Ranch, don't miss the chance for a ride aboard Jones's mule-drawn hay wagon. The bouncing journey takes visitors across open expanses of fields and past a Cherokee Indian cemetery studded with towering cedar trees. Markers date to the late 1800s.

Married for more than a half century, Jones, the father of eight, likes to share his mountain with visitors. His newest offerings include overnight camp-outs, during which visiting dudes can head out on horseback for two to five days away from the ranch.

The only bad thing about a visit here is that eventually the time comes to leave behind the chirping crickets and singing birds. Sooner or later the real world calls—except, of course, for Jack Jones, who gets to stay behind on this mountain-top that he has loved most of his life.

Costs for overnight stays at Shady Grove Dude Ranch vary depending on which facility you choose. Both the Dude Ranch and nearby Cloudmont are often booked for group gatherings and family reunions. For some activities, such as a mealtime trail ride, a minimum group is required. Hayrides, trail meals, and horseback rides are priced separately.

Cloudmont Ski and Golf Resort is about 3 miles from Mentone on DeKalb County Road 89. The Dude Ranch is just across the valley on top of Lookout Mountain, off Alabama Highway 117.

For information about Shady Grove Dude Ranch or Cloudmont Ski and Golf Resort, call 256/634-4344. For more about DeSoto State Park, call 256/845-5380. For information on the surrounding communities, call the DeKalb County Tourist Association at 256/845-3957.

3 WETTING YOUR HOOK IN ALABAMA
FISHING FACTS

It doesn't take a fisherman long to get hooked on fishing in Alabama, where the waters are full of surprises, including world-record bass, championship crappie, catfish, bream, and panfish.

The **Gulf of Mexico** sparkles off Alabama's warm, sunny beaches that yield prize catches of red snapper, king mackerel, blue marlin, cobia, bonito, tarpon, and sailfish. Plus you can deep-sea fish in the Gulf.

The state is also home to **Weiss Lake**, Crappie Capital of the World, as well as **Eufaula**, the world's Big Bass Capital. So there are reasons to drop a line in Alabama waters every day of the year. The only question is: How long can you stay?

NORTH ALABAMA

The waters of North Alabama draw visitors eager to wet their lines and haul in a record catch.

Bankhead Lake turns and twists for 65 miles, creating more than 400 miles of prime water for largemouth bass, spotted bass, and crappie cover.

Wheeler Lake, Alabama's second largest, is a hotbed for catching crappie, the lake's most popular fish.

Bear Creek Watershed Lakes provide the perfect spots for fishermen who want to experience something new each fishing day. These four lakes abound with largemouth bass and panfish.

Guntersville Lake attracts locals searching for crappie. June willow fly hatches send bluegills into a feeding frenzy, providing excellent fly-fishing for the bream angler.

Neely Henry Lake, which is within walking distance of downtown Gadsden, is the place to reel in crappie, spotted bass, and largemouth bass. Bream and catfish also provide steady action here.

Pickwick Lake offers trophy smallmouth bass. You can also take sauger here in winter months.

Lewis Smith Lake boasts crappie, white bass, and largemouth bass. Saltwater striped bass are stocked here as well.

At **Weiss Lake**, the Crappie Capital of the World, you'll find crappie in the springtime and largemouth and spotted bass as the water warms. Catfish and white bass are plentiful in midsummer. The lake is also home to saltwater stripes.

Wilson Lake is the deepest of the four Tennessee River reservoirs. Famous for smallmouths, the river has yielded a 10 1/2-pound prize catch that held the world record for years.

Inland Lake, an unspoiled, scenic gem, offers good bass and bluegill angling. Stocked with hybrids, this lake also supports a good population of easy-to-catch yellow bass.

CENTRAL ALABAMA

The middle region of the state has more than a dozen areas reputed to be outstanding fishing spots.

Aliceville Lake offers great fishing among its scattered timber.

West Point Lake offers excellent largemouth and hybrid striped bass fishing.

Gainesville Lake has been a bass hot spot since it was flooded in 1978. It winds for miles through river hardwoods and pastureland and is stocked with Florida largemouths, saltwater stripes, and hybrids.

Goat Rock and Oliver Lakes total 4,000 acres. The upper end of Goat Rock, the tailwater of Lake Harding, offers an excellent area for catching bass and hybrid striped bass, as well as catfish, in the spring and early summer. In the fall you can catch largemouth bass and hybrid striped bass at the surface while they feed on schooling shad.

Lake Demopolis features many coves and feeder streams that together account for more than 500 miles of shoreline and 10,000 acres of good sport-fish habitat.

R. L. Harris Reservoir (Lake Wedowee), created in 1982, features hundreds of acres of new cover that harbor large numbers of catchable fish. The lake is stocked with spotted bass, hybrids, and channel cat, as well as bass and bream.

Holt Lake, which is full of twists, turns, and small coves, offers fine bass and crappie fishing in April and May and again in the fall. Bream bite best in the feeder streams during the summer.

Jones Bluff has saltwater striped bass, hybrids, and Florida largemouth bass that have been introduced to an already established population of bass, bream, crappie, and channel catfish.

Lake Jordan offers excitement in spring and fall when 1- to 3-pound bass are common. Crappie fishing is excellent during the spring spawn along the shallower banks of the 6,800-acre lake.

Logan Martin Lake is home to crappie in March and largemouth and spotted bass in April or May. In summer look below Neely Henry Dam for stripers, white and hybrid bass, and catfish.

Lake Mitchell, specifically Hatchett Creek, offers some of the state's best wall-eye fishing.

Lay Lake, which is mostly flood timber, provides prime bass, bream, and crappie habitat.

Lake Tuscaloosa is one of two Alabama lakes that receive large numbers of Florida bass annually to determine whether genetic shifts will take place. This lake produces bream, crappie, spotted bass, and catfish.

Warrior Lake provides bass and crappie, with excellent hybrid striped-bass fishing below Warrior Dam, and chain pickerel in spring and summer.

Yates and Thurlow Lake boast extra-large bream.

Opelika City Lake produces good bass fishing in the spring.

Lake Martin on the Tallapoosa River holds more spotted bass than any other lake in Alabama.

SOUTH ALABAMA

Alabama's southern region also abounds with fishing havens.

Coffeeville and Jackson Lakes, fed by the Tombigbee River, offer bass and crappie fishing. Action peaks for bass and crappie in late March and for bream and catfish in June.

Columbia Lake is famous for its striped bass and hybrids.

Big Creek Lake, a scenic reservoir west of Mobile, harbors crappie, hybrid striped bass, and largemouth bass.

Claiborne Lake yields largemouth bass all spring and bream in late spring and early summer.

Gantt Lake and Point A Lake, which are sister lakes, provide excellent fishing spots for redear sunfish. These lakes also hold largemouth, crappie, and white bass.

Lake Eufaula, perhaps Alabama's most celebrated lake, sits on the Chattahoochee River. Local expert Tom Mann made the lake famous for its trophy largemouths. Crappie fishing here is also excellent.

Miller's Ferry, on the Alabama River, may be home to the largest crappie in the state. This lake produces jumbo crappie, largemouths in the spring, and bream and catfish all summer long.

Lake Shelby, about 200 yards from the Gulf of Mexico and Alabama's beaches, abounds with channel catfish.

Dauphin Island, at the mouth of Mobile Bay, offers great year-round fishing.

Photograph by Milton Fullman

This youngster, fishing from the pier at Gulf State Park in Gulf Shores, has learned the lure of fishing.

Gulf Shores boasts great gulf fishing in the waters that surround this world-class beach resort city. Here you can find every species of game fish available on the northern Gulf Coast. The pier at Gulf State Park provides some good angling.

Mobile Delta, the third largest brackish water estuary in the United States, places second to none when it comes to providing great fishing. Access areas to this region abound along the causeway connecting the east and west sides of Mobile Bay.

Perdido Pass, outlet to the Gulf of Mexico, comes closest of all Gulf ports to the exotic bill-fishing locations. It's no surprise that a fleet of sixty charter boats nestles in the harbor at **Orange Beach**.

For more about lakes and lodging in north Alabama, call Alabama Mountain Lakes Association, 800/648-5381 or 256/350-3500. For details about Gulf Coast waters, call the Alabama Gulf Coast Convention and Visitors Bureau, 800/745-7263 (SAND) or 334/968-7511. For information on other places to fish in Alabama, call the Alabama Bureau of Tourism and Travel, 800/252-2262 (ALABAMA).

For information on fishing licenses, call 334/242-3829.

4 FORT PAYNE

GO NORTH, YOUNG MAN, GO NORTH!

In springtime when Mother Nature issues her clarion call to "come out, come out, wherever you are," you may as well comply. Should you wonder where to head on these warm sunny days, the answer is as easy as driving to DeKalb County, where you can pass a weekend . . . or a lifetime.

Here, nature is at her finest in the spring. In **Little River Canyon**, one of the deepest gorges east of the Rocky Mountains, the waters rush and tumble, with falls at each end. As far as anyone knows, this is the only river in the Western Hemisphere that begins and ends on top of a mountain. People who like to hike, rappel, kayak, and canoe embrace this beautiful site and setting.

You can spend hours in Little River Canyon before heading into **Fort Payne**, where you'll find plenty of other things to do.

The group ALABAMA put this tiny northeast town on the map, if for no other reason than the words of one hit song, "My home's in Alabama, no matter where I lay my head."

With that country hit and countless awards, this country music band has endeared itself not just to music fans worldwide, but also to the folks in Fort Payne. People here refer to the band's members as "the boys" (even though one of the foursome did not grow up in Fort Payne), and they've supported a museum that pays tribute to the group's achievements. The **ALABAMA Fan Club and Museum** offers a brief video, a collection of memorabilia, and a gift shop that sells everything from mugs to T-shirts emblazoned with logos and photos of "the boys."

A visit to Fort Payne should include a stop at the **Fort Payne Depot Museum**. Used as a passenger station from 1891 to 1970, the depot has been converted into a museum with historical displays, including railroad memorabilia, artwork, early farm equipment, pottery, and glass. One area resident willed her fascinating lifelong collection of Indian artifacts to the museum. Also of special interest are the dioramas that were once part of a traveling medicine show.

Outside the depot museum stands a twenty-five-foot tree carved into a totem pole that tells a story with figures of animals and Native Americans.

Across from the depot, the 1889 **Fort Payne Opera House** has been used as a vaudeville playhouse, silent-movie theater, and upholstery shop. Restored and reopened in 1969, it is the state's oldest theater still in use. Tours are by appointment only, but if you are lucky there may be a performance taking place during your visit. Be sure to notice the wall mural that details events of the region's history.

Don't miss the **Big Mill Antique Mall**, housed in a building that dates back to 1889. Expect to find a warehouse with a small deli and consignment antiques.

You might anchor your Fort Payne trip with a stay at **DeSoto State Park**, which has a lodge, cabins, and chalets. (Plan ahead because the cabins and chalets book well in advance.) The park has a swimming pool, tennis courts, horseshoes, a playground, and a restaurant. If you have something a bit more cozy in mind, you can stay in one of the area's several bed-and-breakfasts.

At the north entrance to DeSoto State Park you'll find the **Sallie Howard Memorial Chapel**. The back wall of the structure is a rock that crops out of Lookout Mountain. The chapel is always open for Sunday morning services as well as for personal meditation.

If you pass through nearby **Collinsville** on a Saturday, don't miss **Trade Day**, an event dating to 1950 that draws thousands looking for everything from gamecocks and ducks to food and crafts.

Also don't miss **Buck's Pocket State Park,** a secluded and rugged nature area that sprawls across three counties: DeKalb, Jackson, and Marshall. A sign posted at the

Photograph by Milton Fullman

A huge boulder forms the back wall of the Sallie Howard Memorial Chapel near DeSoto State Park.

entrance calls the area a "haven for defeated politicians," a reference to when former governor "Big Jim" Folsom lost a senate race and announced his plan to go to Buck's Pocket to "lick his wounds." He invited other defeated candidates to join him at his favorite retreat. The park offers facilities for primitive camping only.

For more information call the DeKalb County Tourist Association, 256/845-3957.

5 FAIRHOPE • GRAND HOTEL
A GRAND WEEKEND

Years ago **Point Clear** served as a resort for the South's upper crust. Funny how the more things change, the more they stay the same because that's still the case on this slice of land that juts into Mobile Bay.

Many decades ago **Point Clear Hotel** was the place for social gatherings, balls, and high-stakes poker games. Now reincarnated as **The Grand Hotel**, the resort remains a favorite spot for vacationers who come here to find established traditions amid moss-draped oaks and sprawling magnolias.

Built in 1847 as a rambling, two-story wooden building with forty rooms, the original hotel, once accessible only by boat, served as a gathering place for antebellum Southern society. Visitors called the place "the queen of Southern resorts." Destroyed and rebuilt several times, the hotel today has expanded to include three separate buildings and a cluster of cottages.

During the Civil War, the hotel was used as a hospital. Following the war, on July 4, 1869, it reopened as a hotel, but the kitchen and main building later were destroyed by fire. Although guests escaped unharmed, records of the Civil War soldiers treated here were lost in the blaze. Today a small cemetery, void of markers with names, can be found at the center of the resort's 36-hole golf course.

Despite fires and hurricanes, the classy lady has regathered herself and forged ahead, like Scarlett who vowed never to go hungry again. One such rebound occurred in 1981 when Marriott bought the property and renovated the hotel to include additional guest rooms and a conference center.

Regardless of changes over the years, traditions linger at The Grand, where croquet wickets are jabbed into the lawn and a horseshoe pit sits alongside the shore. Tea is served in the main lobby every afternoon, and home-baked cookies are available. Visitors gather to enjoy the goodies before slipping away for a quiet stroll along Mobile Bay.

Two of The Grand's grandest traditions are employees Bucky Miller and Chester Hunt, who have been at the hotel since the early 1940s. Count on Miller to remember your name from visit to visit and to serve one mean Mint Julep!

The resort's 34-slip marina provides easy access to Mobile Bay's waters for guests interested in boating and fishing. Full facilities and docking privileges are available to hotel guests, who may also choose from a selection that includes catamarans, windsurfers, and aqua bikes. Those who prefer a slower pace can relax at the hotel's 750,000-gallon swimming pool.

Although The Grand Hotel, only forty-five minutes from the airport, may seem isolated, it is close to several charming hamlets. Spanish Fort, Daphne, Fairhope, Montrose, and Point Clear dot the nearby coastline and offer year-round golf, boating, and fishing. The area is rife with history, cultural activities, museums, theater productions, and concerts.

Fairhope is noted for its charm, miles of public beaches, a public pier, diverse downtown shopping, art shows, crafts festivals, and theater.

Time seems to have stood still in the quiet Mobile Bay town of Fairhope.

Photograph by Milton Fullman

Point Clear, which became a resort community after the Civil War, has a historic district with several homes built between 1850 and 1930.

A trip to Point Clear would not be complete without a stop at **Punta Clara's Candy Kitchen.** Housed in an 1897 Victorian home known as Miss Colleen's house, this business has been family operated for more than thirty-five years. You'll find exquisite candies, preserves, and other specialties. Warning: Don't take a calorie counter with you.

For more about the Eastern Shore, call the Eastern Shore Chamber of Commerce at 334/928-6387. For details about The Grand Hotel, call 800/544-9933.

6 HIKING
HAPPY TRAILS TO YOU

One year when one of my girls was still wide-eyed and saw every day as a new adventure, she said something that comes back to me each spring. She looked out our picture window at the trees that all winter had been starkly barren and yelled, "Look!" We all rushed to see the cause of her excitement.

Pointing out the window, she announced, "Something's stuck to the trees!"

The "something" stuck to the trees were buds—the promise of leaves, the promise that spring had come at last.

My daughter had shed new light on spring that returns every year.

When springtime arrives, the outdoors beckons. And when it does, there's no better place to be than in Alabama, a state crisscrossed with nature trails—some easy, some tough, some marked, some not. Whether you don your hiking boots to discover sand dunes or shoals, you'll have plenty of choices in Alabama, which once billed itself as "the state of surprises."

Pick the weekend and head in any direction. Pack a few essentials and hike one of the state's many trails. Here is a look, traveling from north to south, at some of Alabama's most popular hiking areas.

NORTH ALABAMA

Muscle Shoals Reservation features trails that are short and relatively easy.

Sipsey River Recreation Area in North Alabama's **Bankhead Forest** sports a network of trails that lace its 25,000 acres. The trails are well marked and challenging.

Joe Wheeler State Park, one of the state's best resorts, has trails that are short and easy.

Honeycomb Creek Trail on **Guntersville Reservoir** provides a pleasant place to hike, with trails that skirt the lake and offer peeks at a variety of waterfowl.

Lake Guntersville State Park has trails both easy and difficult.

At **Buck's Pocket State Park** trails range in difficulty. The largest challenge is the boulder that overlooks this pocket of wilderness not too far from Lake Guntersville.

Lookout Mountain Trail promises to be one of the South's longest and most scenic trails, stretching from Noccalula Falls in Etowah County, across a corner of Georgia for some 100 miles north, to Chattanooga's Lookout Mountain at **Chickamauga National Military Park**. This hike is filled with unusual rock formations and plants, striking views, and waterfalls.

Noccalula Falls Park offers a moderately easy nature trail and a setting worth the visit, whether you hike or not.

Monte Sano State Park, at the eastern boundary of Huntsville, has several trails that range from $1^1/_2$ to $5^1/_2$ miles in length.

The **Madison County Nature Trail** circles a 17-acre lake and serves as a sanctuary for North Alabama plants and wildlife.

River Mont Cave Historic Trail showcases the state's diverse terrain.

DeSoto State Park has signs that identify most of its trails. The most difficult of these is the 7-mile Little River Canyon Trail, which is not for the faint of heart.

Palisades Park near Oneonta provides short, easy, interlinking trails, plus some grand rocks for rappelling.

Point Mallard Park on the banks of the Tennessee River has a 3-mile paved trail that's easy enough for most any walker.

CENTRAL ALABAMA

Lake Chinnabee Recreation Area, in Talladega National Forest close to Cheaha State Park and Pinhoti Trail, has a fairly easy trail that circles a lake.

Cheaha Wilderness Area, in Talladega National Forest, is a favorite among those who prefer rugged and rocky terrain.

Cheaha State Park, at the highest point in Alabama, has well-marked trails that range from easy to moderately strenuous.

Pinhoti National Recreation Trail System is one of the state's longest and most often used. Jutting cliff overhangs demand careful attention.

Horseshoe Bend National Military Park Nature Trail winds around gun placements on a former battlefield.

Bartram Trail in Tuskegee National Forest is simple enough for most any hiker.

Chewacla State Park, within cycling distance of Auburn University, has trails that are sometimes steep but not too long.

Wind Creek State Park, primarily a boating and water recreation area, has several places to traipse about.

Payne Lake Recreation Area in the west-central portion of the state has a small but easily walked trail system.

Lake Lurleen State Park provides a series of hilly hiking trails.

Moundville Archaeological Park, one of the state's most intriguing prehistoric areas, has a 1-mile trail, a museum, and Indian mounds. Boardwalks are being added.

Ruffner Mountain Nature Center, with some 500 acres located east of Birmingham, has three trails that showcase area wildlife and geology.

Oak Mountain State Park has 42 miles of well-marked, interlocking trails.

Rickwood Caverns State Park includes a 1-mile cavern trail and a $1/4$-mile trail connecting the picnic area and **Loop Nature Trail.**

Tannehill Ironworks Historical State Park includes short and easy trails, several of which can accommodate wheelchairs.

SOUTH ALABAMA

The Eufaula National Wildlife Refuge has a 5-mile trail as well as a $1/2$-mile trail, both offering views of wildlife and waterfowl.

Lakepoint Resort State Park has easy and short trails in an area geared for camping, fishing, boating, and hunting.

Conecuh National Forest offers four trails that wind for some 20 easy-going miles. Beware of the alligators.

Gulf Shores State Park has five level, well-marked trails.

Chickasabogue Park provides both wilderness canoe trails and nature trails in the heart of Mobile County.

For details about the state's trails and wilderness areas, call the Alabama Bureau of Tourism and Travel at 800/ALABAMA (252-2262). *Alabama Trails,* by Patricia Stenger Sharpe (published by The University of Alabama Press), also provides useful information.

7 JASMINE HILL
A GARDEN OF LOVE

*You see, I remember when you were born just across the
street, 'cause I was two years old and you just a little old girl
baby. There was a lot of commotion and excitement about your
entry into our neighborhood. Then I watched you grow tall and
most divinely fair, and we married since when you have been ...
my guiding star for fifty-eight blessed years.*

Love, Ben

Inside the cottage at **Jasmine Hill Gardens** this framed letter hangs on the wall.
Most visitors stop to read the scrawl, penned in November 1965 by a man who
loved a woman and whose love helped transform something plain into something beautiful.

Maybe that's what love is about—changing the ordinary into the extraordinary,
the simple into the sublime.

While the letter is not the focus of a visit to Jasmine Hill in Wetumpka, it is the
very essence of why this garden wonderland exists. On a single piece of paper Ben
Fitzpatrick makes it clear that he is in love with his childhood sweetheart, Mary
Mapes, the woman who became his bride in 1907.

Fitzpatrick made his fortune in a retail chain of stores operated throughout the
South. With timing that eluded most others of his generation, the young businessman, in his fourth decade of life, sold his stores. He beat the Great Depression by
a couple of years and kept a promise to his wife to retire early.

One Sunday in the 1920s the Fitzpatricks picnicked with family members in the
shallow hills of Elmore County. On an Alabama hilltop the couple became enchant-
ed with the woodland and a small house badly in need of repair. Having never
become parents, the Fitzpatricks poured their energies and love into this stretch of
woodland in the foothills of the Appalachians.

This area that became their lives' devotion is now open to the public. With addi-
tions the old house became a virtual estate, small but majestic in its surroundings.
Under Mary's guidance in the dozen acres that were to become the heart of Jasmine
Hill Gardens, flower beds became pools, and grown-over fields became lush lawns.
They converted the side yard into a formal garden patterned after its twin at the
Metropolitan Museum, complete with a Roman pool.

Although Mary began with no overall plan, she masterminded a parklike design, merging a series of separate landscape units to form the cohesive Jasmine Hill. She selected plants with the idea that there would be no seasons at Jasmine Hill—something would always be in bloom. The state's mild climate ensures that there is always color here.

In springtime white, pink, and red azaleas line garden walkways. Flowering dogwoods and redbud flourish in the sparsely wooded areas between the pools and fountains. The pools' quiet waters reflect daffodils nestled amidst iris from Spain, tulips from Holland, flowering almond from Japan, and Egyptian lotus.

Photograph by Milton Fullman

Replicas of Greek statues fill Jasmine Hill Gardens, just north of Montgomery.

As May turns to June the fiery sun intensifies the fragrance of gardenias and huge hydrangeas. The constant blooms of crepe myrtle, wisteria, and broad carpets of verbena thrive here in summer.

Flowers, trees, ponds, and walkways are not all that the couple added to their kingdom. Traveling to Greece twenty times in thirty years, they collected reproductions of statues. Ben and Mary would buy a statue and then build a walkway and add more plants and flowers. By the time Ben died in 1969 they had gathered forty statues, a full-size replica of the Temple of Hera, a painted wrought-iron fence, and wall plaques copied from the Italian artist Della Robbia.

After Ben's death his widow remained at Jasmine Hill where, in time, she convinced Jim and Elmore Inscoe to take over the project.

A homespun garden, Jasmine Hill is not grand. It does, however, knit together parallel paths, meandering walkways, open fields, and unexpected enclosures. Always leading onward, the paths lure thousands who visit annually to explore the Fitzpatrick's labor of love.

Not far from Jasmine Hill you can visit **Fort Toulouse-Jackson Park,** site of two forts that were built in different centuries. A visitors center displays silver earrings, French wine bottles, and cannonballs unearthed in the park during archaeological digs. The site's original French fort, dating to 1717, was a trading post where Native Americans exchanged furs and deerskins for European goods. Later, General Andrew Jackson's forces built a nineteenth-century counterpart when they fought the Creeks. The park has a picnic area and campgrounds.

Photograph by Milton Fullman

A statue of a maiden stands majestically in Jasmine Hill Gardens.

Jasmine Hill, on U.S. 231 north of Montgomery, is open year-round Tuesday through Sunday. Walking-tour brochures are available. Staff-guided tours can be arranged for an additional fee. Admission is charged. Take a picnic to Jasmine Hill and lunch on the grounds. For details call Jasmine Hill at 334/567-6463.

Nineteen miles west of Montgomery you can enjoy a driving tour of **Lowndesboro,** once a prosperous antebellum village near a bend in the Alabama River. Incorporated in 1832, the town was home to wealthy cotton farmers who built stately houses and shops along the main road. Although the cotton-based economy failed to rebound following the Civil War, the town's churches and pre-Civil War houses remain.

In Prattville, a couple of dozen miles west of Wetumpka, explore **Prattvillage** and its restored nineteenth-century buildings and houses. The historic **Mims**

Photograph by Milton Fullman

Canopied by trees and outlined with flowers, a path leads •
visitors into a garden wonderland in Wetumpka.

Hotel, moved to Prattvillage in 1982, was home to the poet Sidney Lanier while he taught in the area. In downtown Prattville visit the **Prattaugan Museum** to see historic documents and memorabilia from Autauga County's early years. Roam through **Wilderness Park**, a natural forest inside the city limits of Prattville. Appoximately one half mile, the trail is easy walking for visitors of all ages. Don't miss **Buena Vista**, an elegant antebellum mansion (Tour times at Buena Vista are limited, so check before going.)

For information about Prattville call the chamber of commerce at 334/365-7392.

8 MOBILE

A TOWN UNLIKE ANY OTHER

Mobile, with its moss-draped trees, gulf waters brushing its shorelines, and history reaching back a couple hundred years, is unique among Alabama cities.

Here, where Alabama meets the sea, you will find historic districts, water sports, museums, a retired battleship, restored forts, and enough azaleas to fill a rack of postcards.

The warmth of the sun beating down on this South Alabama city year-round reflects the warmth of residents' smiles and greetings of welcome.

Begin your visit at **Fort Conde**, Mobile's official welcome center. In the early 1700s, the site's original fort served as headquarters for the French Louisiana Territory.

Early in your visit make your way to the **City Museum** in the **Bernstein–Bush House**. This Italianate townhouse, sitting on an oak-lined city street, includes Mardi Gras and Civil War exhibits, antique carriages, and other items detailing the city's past.

Photograph by Milton Fullman

At Battleship Park on Mobile Bay, visitors have the chance to explore the submarine USS Drum, berthed alongside the USS Alabama.

Within walking distance of the museum you'll find the **Phoenix Fire Museum**, which showcases turn-of-the-century steam engines and other fire-fighting equipment, mementos, and tools.

The annual **Azalea Trail Festival** is one of Mobile's noted events. Along with music, art, and theater, this springtime event allows the city to showcase its miles of pink, blossom-lined streets.

Plantings made years ago by the city have given Mobile its reputation as azalea capital of the world. In just five years

23

the 4,000 azalea bushes planted in 1929 multiplied to 38,000 bushes. The azalea explosion has continued.

Mobile's downtown has made a comeback, and **Dauphin Street** has emerged as a downtown hot spot with shops and places to find food and entertainment. While you're there, try the fried pizza and beer sausage at **Port City Brewery.**

Cathedral Square, not far from downtown, faces the **Cathedral of the Immaculate Conception.** The parklike square has become the centerpiece of a four-teen-block arts district. Jazz festivals, art exhibits, and the city's annual New Year's celebration, called **First Night,** take place here. First Night offers live entertainment, foods, storytelling, skits, and puppet shows. Alcohol is not permitted at these events.

Adding to the appeal of the comeback downtown are many museums and historic homes that trace the city's history. These attractions include some of Alabama's most elegant and historic houses—the **Conde-Charlotte House, Oakleigh,** the **Richards-DAR House,** and the **Bragg-Mitchell Mansion.** Restored and converted into museums, these houses offer a glimpse into the city's early years.

Nature is at her best in **Mobile Botanical Gardens,** 64 acres that include a nature trail and an extensive collection of azaleas. The Gardens also include a self-guided nature trail and texture garden.

Be sure to see **Bienville Square,** an azalea-studded park canopied by live oaks. The park comes to life during Christmas, when thousands of white lights twinkle in the trees. Take along some peanuts and you're sure to be a hit with the resident squirrels.

Photograph by Milton Fullman

Modern history is preserved 1 mile east of Mobile at the **USS Alabama Battleship Memorial Park,** a 100-acre site showpiecing the decommissioned battleship that was launched in 1942. The park also includes the **USS Drum,** military aircraft and equipment, hundreds of varieties of roses, a boardwalk, and a two-story observation deck that provides a view of Southern wetlands.

The raised-cottage style Oakleigh Mansion is one of Mobile's most important antebellum house museums.

Framed by slender, fluted columns, the Bragg-Mitchell Mansion today is open to the public.

Life here is abundant, but never more so than at the annual **Mardi Gras** celebration. Although New Orleans is best known for its Mardi Gras celebrations, Mobile has celebrated the occasion longer than any other U.S. city.

Spend a weekend in Mobile, and you'll come away convinced that Alabama's second largest city overflows with charm, hospitality, grace, history, and tradition. Stay downtown to be within walking distance of many of the city's sites. Chain hotels are well represented, plus there is **Malaga Inn,** a small inn built around matching Italianate houses.

For more information about Mobile, call Mobile Tourism and Travel at 800/ 5-MOBILE (662453).

9 SELMA
SEARCHING SELMA

Selma is one of Alabama's quiet, small cities—or so it might seem at first glance. During the Civil War Selma served as one of the South's main military manufacturing centers, turning out Confederate warships, including the ironclad *Tennessee*. In 1865 the town was the site of what is said to have been the war's final battle.

One hundred years after the Civil War battle, another conflict would upstage the war and become the most memorable event in the city's history. It was in Selma that Dr. Martin Luther King Jr. staged his encounter with the racist voting regulations of the South. The Selma-to-Montgomery Voting Rights March was intended to be a nonviolent, symbolic march, but things turned out much differently. On Sunday, March 7, 1965, the march plans went awry. The national media was on hand to record "Bloody Sunday." This event drew national attention, and hundreds of sympathizers vowing to help with the civil rights struggle poured into Selma.

As reminders of those protests the folks in Selma annually reenact the march across **Edmund Pettus Bridge**. A bronze statue of King stands in front of **Brown Chapel AME Church**, midpoint on the city's historic walking tour along Martin Luther King Jr. Street.

The men, women, and children who participated during the 1960s in the civil rights struggle are recognized at the **National Voting Rights Museum**, located in a historic building in the city's riverfront district two doors down

A rear window of the National Voting Rights Museum looks onto the Edmund Pettus Bridge, known for its role in the Selma-to-Montgomery March.

Photograph by Milton Fullman

26

Photograph by Milton Fullman

Selma's old depot has been transformed into a museum showcasing relics from the city's early years.

from the foot of Edmund Pettus Bridge. The museum displays portraits of distinguished leaders from the Reconstruction period. It also houses a women's suffrage room that showcases portraits of such women as Sojourner Truth, Harriet Tubman, and Ida B. Wells.

A mirrored wall in the museum's entranceway entitled "I Was There" is splattered with tiny notes scrawled by visitors who took part in the march on Bloody Sunday. In their own handwriting, with words like "scared" and "hurt," they have recorded their memories of a day that changed the course of our nation.

With the state's largest historic district, Selma preserves much of its history in the **Old Depot Museum,** a former train station filled with mementos of the men and women who helped to make Selma the "Queen City of the Black Belt." Exhibits range from items as large as a railroad boxcar to those as small as the black pins worn by nineteenth-century ladies in mourning dress. The museum also displays William Rufus King's china and silver service, used when he served as ambassador to France, and a cameo brooch that belonged to Selma resident Elodie Todd Dawson, a half-sister of Abraham Lincoln's wife.

Not far away a majestic era of the city's history is recalled at **Sturdivant Hall,** one of the finest Greek Revival mansions in the South. Now a museum housing antiques, period furniture, and portraits, the ten-room house was completed in 1853 by architect Thomas Helm Lee, a cousin of General Robert E. Lee.

"People come here thinking they will see a few antebellum homes, but Selma has street after street of antebellum houses," said Jamie Wallace, president of the Selma-Dallas County Chamber of Commerce.

The people here take seriously their duty to preserve their past, much of which is on view in the **Smitherman Historic Building.** Originally a school, the building later served as a Confederate hospital and then as the Dallas County Courthouse. Today the building houses the **Art Lewis Civil War collection,** furniture, and displays of Selma's history.

While you're in Selma, don't miss the chance to ramble through **Siegel Gallery,** housed in an 1840 Greek Revival cottage that originally stood in old Cahawba. Here you'll find an outstanding collection of national, regional, and local art.

Martin Luther King Jr., looking back at the civil rights struggles staged here, once observed: "Confrontation of good and evil compressed in the tiny community of Selma generated the massive power to turn the whole nation to a new course."

What happened in those earlier years is not what matters the most, however. What matters most is that Selma, its people, and the world have learned from the events that took place here.

Each spring Selma opens selected homes for pilgrimage. **The Battle of Selma** is remembered on April's fourth full weekend in the state's largest Civil War commemoration, complete with authentic encampments and nighttime artillery firing exhibitions. For more information call the Selma-Dallas County Chamber of Commerce's Tourism Division at 800/45-SELMA (73562) or 334/875-7241.

10 TANNEHILL IRONWORKS HISTORICAL STATE PARK
FUN, FOOD, AND FURNACES

C all it cabin fever if you want, but in the springtime I have one single thought: Thank goodness winter's cold is slipping away. With the passing of winter I get an irresistible urge to leave fireplaces and central heat. I want to be outdoors. I want to touch a tree, search for budding flowers. Winter and that dreadful disease—cabin fever—take their toll.

Fortunately **Tannehill Ironworks Historical State Park,** a 1,500-acre historical complex at the corners of Jefferson, Tuscaloosa, and Bibb Counties offers an escape. Once the ironworks' natural concealment, the dense forests here are now penetrated by self-guided scenic trails.

Tannehill's history dates to 1830, when iron was first manufactured here. In those early days Tannehill was a community in itself, with a blacksmith shop, gristmill, sawmill, tannery, and living quarters for the furnace workers.

The Confederate government added two more furnaces in 1863, and those became major suppliers for the Confederate Army. Each day the furnaces produced more than 20 tons of pig iron used to make cannonballs, gun barrels, and other munitions. Tannehill Ironworks, along with a handful of other Alabama furnaces, was producing seventy percent of the Confederate iron.

Something this important to the Confederate Army, however, did not go unnoticed. The Union Army targeted the furnace. On March 20, 1865, Union Major General James H. Wilson, with 14,000 seasoned troops, stormed into the heart of Alabama, intending to destroy the industrial heart of the Confederacy. Tannehill was the primary target.

Photograph by Milton Fullman

Friends savor a sunny day on a creek bank at Tannehill Ironworks Historical State Park.

29

Shortly after daybreak on March 31, three Union companies struck the undefended ironworks. Forewarned, workers had taken refuge in nearby woods. Within minutes Tannehill was in flames. A week later General Robert E. Lee surrendered, ending the Civil War.

For decades it seemed as though this piece of Southern history was lost forever. Then in 1969, after sitting abandoned for almost a century, the furnaces received new life when the Alabama Legislature established Tannehill Ironworks Historical State Park as a state memorial to the history of iron and steel manufacturing in Alabama.

An escape to Tannehill is more than a chance to escape hearth and home. It's also a chance to step back in time.

Along with its restored ironworks, the farm, and more than forty-five structures—all dating to the 1800s—were moved to Tannehill from the four corners of the state.

Farm life is re-created at **Tannehill Farm**, which includes a working blacksmith shop, a sorghum mill, the 1850 **Williams House**, and a barn dating to 1822.

Also at the farm you'll see **John Wesley Hall's Mill**, a gristmill and cotton gin that operated from 1867 to 1931. The mill was restored in the late 1970s and continues to turn out cornmeal for park visitors.

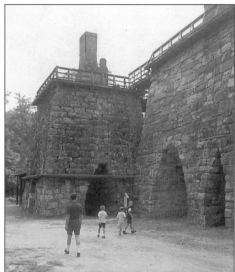

Photograph by Milton Fullman

Old furnaces, which once produced munitions for Confederate troops, are a centerpiece at Tannehill.

While at the park be sure to see the **Iron and Steel Museum of Alabama**, which displays the South's largest collection of ironworks artifacts. Exhibits and photographs trace the history of the area from the time of the Creek Indians, who used the iron to make arrowheads.

Not far from the museum you will find the restored furnaces. In 1976, Furnace No. 1 roared back to life with a 3,100-degree blast. Within a week more than two tons of pig iron had been produced. The restorations at Tannehill represent the first time a Civil War–era ironworks has been put back on blast after being silent for more than a century.

The countryside in Tannehill is laced with historic trails, some meandering along creek banks, all punctuated with wildlife and forest flowers. These trails provide an irresistible opportunity to see and touch springtime.

The park, 12 miles south of Bessemer off I-59, is open daily. The museum and **Furnace Master's Restaurant** are closed major holidays; the restaurant, which serves home-cooked foods, is also closed Mondays. Modest admission is charged for park entrance.

Campers have access to some 200 improved campsites, with electrical and water hookups and three modern bathhouses. An additional fifty sites are available to tent campers. For information call 205/477-5711.

Photograph by Milton Fullman

Much to the delight of youngsters, a mini-train crawls through the wooded state park just west of Birmingham.

1 AUBURN • OPELIKA • TUSKEGEE
WAR EAGLE AND OTHER STUFF

Despite common belief, there is more to Auburn than a sprawling college campus and a great football team. By "hubbing" a weekend in this town, you can do everything from fish and explore museums to search for ghosts and plunge down a waterslide.

You can begin your explorations of this eastern Alabama region by checking in at the **Auburn University Hotel and Conference Center**, which offers a variety of package rates at a convenient location.

If youngsters are along, unpack your swimsuits and head first to **Surfside Water Park**. At Exit 51 off I-85, the park has picnic areas, a snack bar, volleyball courts, a video arcade, children's pool, and a play area. A pool with gentle waves and an honest-to-goodness sandy beach will make you think you're at the ocean. There's also a lazy river where kids and adults can walk, float, and glide to beat the pounding heat. And for the bold of spirit there are four body flumes and two speed slides that send riders plunging. The park, just south of Auburn, is open daily Memorial Day through Labor Day.

Next door, Chewacla State Park's 700 acres and 26-acre lake offer other outdoor options including picnic tables and shelters, a playground, a lakefront beach, supervised swimming, fishing, RV and tent campsites, and a few cabins that book rapidly. (Cabins require a two-night stay on weekends and three nights on holidays.) You can rent rowboats, canoes, and paddleboats by the hour year-round.

Once you've dried off, tour "The Plains," otherwise known as Auburn. Be sure to stop for lemonade at **Toomer's Drugstore**, diagonally across the street from the main entrance to the university campus. Browse through **Johnston-Malone Bookstore**, where collegiates spend their parents' money on everything from used books to Auburn souvenirs.

Photograph by Milton Fullman

Photograph by Milton Fullman

(Left) On the campus of Tuskegee Institute, a museum remembers institute founder Booker T. Washington and scientist George Washington Carver.
(Right) A statue of Booker T. Washington lifting the veil of ignorance from a fellow African-American is a favorite meeting spot on the Tuskegee Institute campus.

Check out the campus chapel, which dates back to 1850 and was used as a Civil War hospital. This Gothic Revival–style church is said to be haunted, so stick around long enough to search for the lingering spirit, supposedly associated with a Civil War soldier. And don't miss **Jordan-Hare Stadium,** home of the Auburn Tigers, which seats more than 85,000 fans and roars with excitement on fall game days.

Head next to Opelika to tour the **Whitfield-Searcy House,** now home of the Opelika Chamber of Commerce. This Queen Anne–style house has gables, banjo work around the outside, and a widow's walk on top.

Seven miles west of Auburn on Alabama Highway 14, you will find several structures in the Loachapoka Historic District dating to the mid-1800s that can be toured by foot or by car. The **Lee County Historical Society Museum,** housed in the old Trading Center building, displays a collection of artifacts and memorabilia relating to the county. Don't miss the restored log cabin, blacksmith shop, cookhouse, and the large building that displays farm tools.

Set aside a segment of your weekend to visit Tuskegee, about 15 miles south of Auburn on the eastern end of the state's Black Belt in Macon County. Central to the city's heritage is **Tuskegee University**, which originated in a dilapidated church and shanty in the summer of 1881.

Spend at least one hour touring the **Carver Museum**, a visitor-orientation center housed in a brick building that was originally used as a laundry. There you can view films that detail the lives of scientist George Washington Carver, educator Booker T. Washington, and the men who developed this institute into one of the nation's most respected African-American colleges.

Born a slave, Carver overcame adverse beginnings to earn a master's degree from Iowa Agricultural College and to become a recognized leader in agricultural research. Highlights in the museum include the preserved vegetable specimens and samples of products made from peanuts and sweet potatoes, the two crop plants that Carver studied extensively. Before the turn of the century Carver developed 300 extractions from peanuts and 175 by-products from sweet potatoes.

Up the hill from the museum you can visit the home of Booker T. Washington, who was the first principal of Tuskegee State Normal School. Called "**The Oaks**," the house is a two-story, fifteen-room structure built by Tuskegee students. Washington lived there until his death in 1915.

Not far from the museum is the Booker T. Washington monument, which depicts Washington lifting the veil of ignorance shrouding fellow African Americans. Across from the monument stands **University Chapel**, completed in 1963 to replace the original chapel

Photograph by Milton Fullman

At Chewacla State Park, a 26-acre lake includes a lakefront beach.

Photograph by Milton Fullman

Near Auburn, Surfside Water Park is a grand place to cool off on a hot summer day.

destroyed by fire. Near the chapel are the gravesites of Booker T. Washington and others associated with the university's history and development.

Don't leave without driving through the campus district, which includes 165 buildings, 27 of which have historical significance.

A few miles northeast of the campus is **Moton Field,** which has been called the "Cradle of Black Aviation." During World War II Tuskegee and the Army Air Corps conducted primary pilot training for African-American officers. Moton Field became the only place in the United States where African Americans could train as military pilots.

Tuskegee National Forest, off U.S. 29, is the state's smallest national forest. It contains a walking trail and native plants but no campsites. If you plan to camp while visiting this region along the Chattahoochee Trace, try the RV campsites adjacent to Surfside Water Park in Auburn. These are equipped with power, water, and sewage hookups, as well as cable TV connections. Ice machines, a laundry room, vending machines, and a bathhouse with showers are also available, and tent camping is permitted.

Once you've explored this region that snuggles up to the Georgia border, you may want to plan a return trip in the fall to watch the Auburn Tigers wage battle on their gridiron. Remember to wear orange and blue. And come prepared to bellow—to everyone and no one in particular—the cry so often heard in The Plains: "War Eagle!"

Photograph by Milton Fullman

Gliding lazily down a man-made river is one of the simple pleasures at Surfside Water Park.

For more information about Auburn, call the Auburn–Opelika Convention and Visitors Bureau, 800/321-8880 or 334/887-8747.

For more about Chewacla State Park, call 800/ALA-PARK (252-7275) or 334/887-5621.

For more about Tuskegee call the Alabama Bureau of Tourism and Travel, 800/ALABAMA (252-2262).

2 BIRMINGHAM BARONS
TAKE ME OUT TO THE BALL GAME

Summer wouldn't be summer without baseball, and Alabama has its share of players, games, and diamond duels.

The **Birmingham Barons** have entertained fans since the city's early years. In those days the team played at a slag pile where only 600 spectators could fit in the grandstand. Those who didn't arrive early enough to get seats perched atop slag piles behind the outfield fence. That crude beginning in 1885 was a far cry from the modern stadium where the Chicago White Sox's AA team plays today.

The Barons play their seventy home games at the **Hoover Met**, a stadium that became their home in spring 1988 after decades of games at historic Rickwood Field. Sitting south of Birmingham, The Met seats 10,800.

Watching the team is akin to watching tomorrow's rising stars. Through the years the Barons roster has included the names of 1993–94 American League Most Valuable Player Frank Thomas, 1993 Cy Young Award winner Jack McDowell, and Bo Jackson.

Photograph courtesy of Birmingham Convention and Visitors Bureau

A Birmingham Barons game is a good place to spot stars on the rise to the big leagues.

Six players from the pages of Birmingham Barons history have been elected to the Baseball Hall of Fame in Cooperstown, New York: Burleigh Grimes, a Baron from 1914 to 1916; Pie Traynor, in 1921; Satchel Paige, from 1927 to 1930; Willie Mays, from 1948 to 1950; Reggie Jackson, in 1967; and Rollie Fingers, from 1967 to 1968.

The Riverchase Galleria, just south of Birmingham, is a virtual city under glass.

Even the greats pale in comparison though to the 1994 arrival of NBA superstar Michael Jordan, who was assigned to the Barons when, for a period, he switched from basketball to baseball. Jordan's popularity helped shatter all existing club attendance records.

The king-of-courts' performance with the Barons was so widely observed that billboards were erected to tout his current batting average. When all was said and done, it was a very good year for the basketball standout who batted .202, with 3 homers, 51 runs batted in, and 30 stolen bases, while the club was covered by journalists from around the world.

The Barons, who open their season each April and play their final game in early fall, consider their games and surrounding fanfare some of Birmingham's finest family entertainment. Home games often include giveaways and special events such as a diamond dig or complimentary helmets and batting gloves.

To get to the Hoover Met from I-65 or U.S. 280, take I-459 toward Tuscaloosa. Go past the Riverchase Galleria to Exit 10 (Highway 150), and follow the signs.

For a family of four, the cost of a game, hot dog, and soft drink is in the $25 range. For information about the Barons schedule, contact the Birmingham Barons Baseball Club, P.O. Box 360007, Birmingham, AL 35236; 205/988-3200.

When fans aren't at games, they can shop until they drop at nearby **Riverchase Galleria,** one of the Southeast's largest shopping meccas. Anchored by J.C. Penney, Macy's, McRae's, Parisian, Rich's, and Sears, the complex has some 200 specialty stores and a sprawling food court. The Galleria is connected to the Wynfrey Hotel, which offers special packages for shoppers.

To round out a Barons weekend, investigate nearby attractions such as the **Shelby County Museum and Archives.** On Main Street in Columbiana, the museum is housed in a restored courthouse that dates to circa 1854.

The Smith Harrison Museum, in the Mildred Harrison Regional Library just east of the Shelby County Courthouse, boasts the largest collection of George and Martha Washington memorabilia outside Mount Vernon.

Also convenient to The Met is the **Bessemer Hall of History,** which is listed on the National Register of Historic Places. Housed in the renovated **Southern Railway Depot,** the collection chronicles the history of Bessemer, Jefferson County, and Alabama.

A bust of Martha Washington is included in the collection at the Smith Harrison Museum in Columbiana.

Photograph by Milton Fullman

Oak Mountain State Park, off I-65 just 10 miles south of Birmingham, is the largest park in the state's system. Here you can golf, fish, camp, hike, bike, and boat on some 10,000 acres. The park also has a petting zoo—a favorite with young visitors.

Five Points South provides great people-watching, dancing, nightspots, and wonderful meals in the city's entertainment district. Stroll tree-lined streets or stop at the fountain to admire the artistry of Frank Fleming's sculpture "**The Storyteller.**"

For more information about Birmingham, call the Greater Birmingham Convention and Visitors Bureau at 800/458-8085 or 205/458-8000.

3 CHILDERSBURG

A PARK FOR A LARK

I watched the two children in front of me as I started my descent into **DeSoto Caverns** in Childersburg. The boy was maybe eight, and his pigtailed sister a couple of years younger. Wide-eyed, they clutched their father's hands. I imagined that little could spook these kids of the television/Nintendo generation, but heading into the huge underground cave proved me wrong.

It was dim inside as our guide told us about the cave, owned by a fourth generation of the Mathis family, who have made it one of the state's most heavily promoted tourist attractions. DeSoto Caverns opened to the public in 1965. It became the nation's first officially recorded cave in 1796, when Benjamin Hawkins, general superintendent of Native American Indian tribes south of the Ohio River, wrote to President Washington to detail the cavern's beauty.

The cave's spring-fed well made it the perfect place for Confederate soldiers to mine calcium nitrate, and the caves became a gunpowder mining and refining center. You can see the well and a leaching trough used by the soldiers.

Photograph by Milton Fullman

The entrance to DeSoto Caverns Park heralds the fun that is to come.

41

Learning to shoot a bow and arrow is one activity available on the grounds outside DeSoto Caverns Park.

Native Americans buried their dead here, and moonshiners spent a few years making white lightning while hiding from the law. We also learned that bats occasionally find their way indoors, where the stalagmites and stalactites jut upward and downward as a waterfall creates splashing background sounds. (With this bit of bat news from our guide, the children flinched and huddled closer to their father. Nothing like a good bat story to dampen a youngster's sense of adventure.)

The most dramatic part of the cave tour is the laser light show that begins with a spoof from the guide. "Want to see just how dark it can be inside a cave?" the guide asks, before turning off the lights. Raise your hand to your face, and you see nothing. After a few seconds of darkness, the dramatic light show begins. Although the laser show may seem an anachronism in this place steeped in Native American, Civil War, and Prohibition history, it offers a flare for today's generation accustomed to dramatic effects.

DeSoto Caverns Park, an 80-acre mini-theme park designed for kids, is highlighted by a trip inside the illuminated caverns, where tours take about an hour and include a sound, water, and laser light show in the large onyx chamber. You will enter the cave through an opening in the side of a hill, so be sure to wear functional shoes. Several dozen steps lead deep into the great cathedral room, which is taller than a twelve-story building. The ceiling glows with thousands of yellow, orange, and red stalactites.

Inside the cave entrance, you can see etched in stone the year "1723," said to have been carved by a fur trader named I. W. Wright, who was killed by Native Americans because he had violated their burial grounds.

Named for the Spanish explorer Hernando DeSoto, who visited the area in 1540, the caverns have a year-round indoor temperature of 60 degrees. Onyx formations within the cave bear clever names not too difficult to figure out. For instance, there is a "frozen waterfall" and a "giant's foot." Just for fun, stare at the formations and make up names of your own.

Outside the cave you'll find several attractions. These cost extra but help make the destination one that requires several hours to enjoy. Kids especially like the 3/4-acre maze that takes some clever navigating to conquer. There is also a place to learn to shoot with a bow and arrow as well as a spot to pan for colored stones. (This one is a bit hokey, so let only the youngest in your party participate.) Young boys especially like the Indian teepee versus the Spanish fort, where participants hurl water balloons across a grassy stretch to drench their opponents. Each player gets ten balloons to toss.

There is no restaurant, but food options include sandwiches, french fries, pizza, and corndogs that can be microwaved. Fudge, divinity, and hand-scooped ice cream are also available.

Or you can take along your own picnic and head to one of the surrounding picnic tables, which are plentiful on the meticulously maintained grounds. These tables also are put to good use when school groups visit the park. If you have an RV you may want to stay overnight in the adjacent campgrounds that offer full and partial hookups.

Photograph by Milton Fullman

A man-made mill churns at DeSoto Caverns Park, on the site where early explorers once traipsed.

Several miles from DeSoto Caverns Park is **Kymulga Grist Mill Park**, 78 acres of what has been called the largest cluster of white oak trees east of the Mississippi. Here you can tour an 1864 water-powered mill, that was built by slave labor, which still grinds meal. Locals bring their homegrown kernels here once a week to be ground for a nominal fee. You can purchase meal here.

Kymulga Park includes 2 miles of well-marked hiking trails and a 105-foot covered bridge still open to pedestrian traffic. Dating to the 1860s, the bridge spans Talladega Creek.

Inside a wood-floor country store adjacent to the mill you will find a picture of Franklin Delano Roosevelt with the caption "Thanks for the foresight of Mr. Albert Burton and President Roosevelt, this gristmill still stands."

Here's how it happened: In 1941 the federal government bought 18,000 acres that included the land where the mill stands. The mill was going to be torn down, but Burton wrote to Roosevelt, and the president was persuaded to set aside 2 acres for the mill. Burton, who had only a third-grade education, operated the site's country store for almost three decades.

The mill is still covered on the outside with its original boards, and the same hand-hewn posts and beams continue to support the inside. The floorboards are mostly original, with only a few patches of replacements here and there. Upstairs, vibrations travel through the boards when the old grinding device is set in motion.

If you didn't find time to snack at DeSoto Caverns, take advantage of this Kymulga setting, where weddings often take place under the quiet canopy of towering trees and a pavilion available for special events. You might enjoy picnicking here.

Every year DeSoto Caverns Park hosts an Indian Dance and Country Crafts Festival in April, a September Fest, and a Christmas Festival of Lights daily from Thanksgiving through December.

DeSoto Caverns Park, 36 miles southeast of Birmingham, is open year-round except Thanksgiving and Christmas. For specifics and admission costs, call 256/378-7252.

Kymulga Grist Mill, 256/378-7436, is open daily summer through fall.

For more about Childersburg call the chamber of commerce at 256/378-5482.

4 GULF SHORES • ORANGE BEACH
LOUNGE LIZARDS AND OTHER THINGS FOUND ALONG THE BEACH

An American flag atop the **Flora–Bama Lounge** whips in the breeze that blows from the Gulf of Mexico. The sounds of jazz, country, rock, and blues seep from inside.

Three young men, walking straight as arrows and wearing the dress white of the U.S. Navy, spill from a small car. A couple with sandals and sunburned faces holds hands and heads toward the music. A lone man riding a motorcycle stops and goes toward the door.

A police officer stops traffic along Alabama Highway 182 to allow visitors to descend upon this legendary place, a spot made famous in the 1960s when football great Kenny Stabler proclaimed it "the best watering hole in the country." As someone observed recently, this is the place where you can holler "Bubba" and fifteen people will respond. It's a place where you could wrap your head in toilet paper and nobody would notice or care.

Out front is a package store, but most people go right on past to follow the music and witness the legend. A landmark since the 1960s, this rustic lounge

Photograph by Milton Fullman

Sun worshiping is a main attraction along Alabama's Gulf Coast.

45

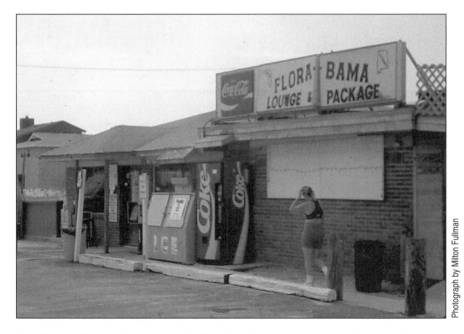

Photograph by Milton Fullman

Straddling the Florida-Alabama border, the Flora-Bama Lounge was immortalized in a 1984 Jimmy Buffett song.

straddles the Alabama–Florida line. Raw wood frames some of the rooms, which are furnished with unmatched tables and chairs and some bar stools scattered here and there.

Out back, beyond a maze of rooms that seem to have been added on by a kid with treehouse-building skills, a boardwalk leads to the beach. Generally though, only the romantic wander that far. It would be a crime somehow to come here and not be a part of the action.

People come here to watch other people. Some dance, some roam outside and inside, then outside again. Others snuggle close at a bar. Some peel boiled shrimp, and a few try to see how much they can imbibe.

You don't visit the Flora–Bama for its looks. You visit because it is a place of world renown, a place that each January holds a Polar Bear Dip and each spring hosts a mullet toss—neither of which is for the weak of heart. Those who gather for the annual January dip jump into the cold Gulf water; only no-guts, no-glory kind of folks need participate. During the spring, when the weather is much more inviting, contestants stand on the Florida side of the beach to see who can throw a mullet farthest into Alabama.

Open every day of the year, the Flora–Bama was immortalized in a 1984 Jimmy Buffett song: "Go on down to the Gulf and listen to some Western music, Gonna get ourselves a cool one at the Flora–Bama." The lounge-turned-tourist-attraction was built in 1964, two years after Florida completed the coast road that connects Perdido Key and Orange Beach. As crowds increased, a back room, side room, and raised room were added. There is no method to the madness, but it doesn't much matter. What matters is that the additions have made space for more people.

Although the Flora–Bama is the area's most noted lounge, there are others, including the **Pink Pony,** which stands at the edge of a boardwalk dotted with places to eat, meet, laugh, and drink. By night these are the places where you'll catch the flavor of the Gulf Coast.

By day one of the best ways to feel this region is on a sailboat. It's simple, actually. Gather whatever you want to take along for a several-hour boat trip and then head to the bay, where numerous businesses sponsor excursions.

I was lucky. After several hours on the boat I was treated to an incredible sunset—a huge ball of orange slipping down, down, down, growing brighter and more orange as it tumbled out of sight.

When rain drizzles and sunshine seems forever removed, I like to remember my sailboat ride at Gulf Shores—the sunset and the breeze that seemed to blow my cares away. And when I want to think of places that make life interesting, I remember nights at the Flora–Bama.

Alabama's 32 miles of beaches appeal especially to those who love nature, the sun, the outdoors, and water sports. Others are drawn by the fresh seafood and places to escape with a good book while lulled by the sounds of the surf. Also inviting are the public beaches with their boardwalks, picnic areas, and bathhouses.

Nature lovers revel in **Bon Secour National Wildlife Refuge**—more than two miles of beachfront accessible by nature trails. Six miles west of Gulf Shores, the 6,200-acre oasis of wildlife at Bon Secour offers fresh- and saltwater fishing along with four miles of walking trails.

The 6,000-acre **Gulf State Park,** which has received Family Circle's prestigious Family Resort of the Year Award, has more than two miles of beach and a long pier that juts into the gulf. Campsites, picnic areas, and boat ramps are available.

Gulf Shores provides a wide array of activities. Beach rental companies along the shore offer jet skis, catamarans, and boogie boards. Just remember to bring a towel, suntan oil and sunscreen, and camera.

More than one hundred boats are available for charter from **Alabama's Deep Sea Fishing Fleet** at Orange Beach. Seasoned captains know where and when the fish are running, and all boats are equipped with electronic fish-finding devices.

For some visitors, sticking to the shore can mean sun worshiping on the sand or exploring the coast on horseback. Off-beach activities include bike and moped rentals as well as plane and helicopter rides.

Families can enjoy miniature golf, up-close wilderness adventures at **Zooland Animal Park,** or the slides and rides of **Waterville, USA.** In addition there is the fast-paced action of **The Track,** a family recreation center.

Because of the coastal area's mild year-round climate, golf is a popular attraction with plenty of places to tee off.

Those who prefer shopping can also stay busy. Souvenir and gift shops abound, interspersed by sportswear and fine fashion boutiques. Just ten minutes from the beach, an outlet mall offers more than a hundred factory stores.

With more than seven thousand hotel, motel, and condominium units, Gulf Shores offers just about every kind of accommodation. Luxury hotels and condominiums stand side-by-side with beach houses—some weathered, some crisp and contemporary. Together the structures paint a horizon that is both homey and inviting.

For a memorable overnight stay in a Casablanca-kind of place, try the **Original Romar House**—one of Orange Beach's landmark structures that has been converted into a bed-and-breakfast. Quality Inn Beachside is another reliable option.

When dining along the coast, take advantage of the fresh seafood. Quaint places to eat include **Bayside Grill at Sportsman Marina** and **Tacky Jack's at Cotton Bayou Marina.** Hazel's has buffets at every meal.

If art interests you, drop by **Rick Tino's Gallery** in Gulf Shores.

For more about Gulf Shores or Orange Beach, contact the Alabama Gulf Coast Convention and Visitors Bureau, P.O. Drawer 457, Gulf Shores, AL 36547; 800/745-SAND (7263) or 334/968-7511.

5 LAKE MARTIN
AND THE LIVING IS EASY

The sun settles over the lake as a tiny ripple grows wider and wider, hinting at where a bass has just looped from the deeper waters. Sounds of talk and laughter echo across the lake as whippoorwills present their evening cantatas. Only the occasional roar of a boat zipping past shatters the peaceful calm.

Lake Martin is a product of man's ingenuity and a corporation's grand dam that spread water over what was once a tiny farming community. The village, which had been evacuated or relocated, drowned in 1926 when the Tallapoosa River began backing up after completion of the $20-million Martin Dam built by Alabama Power. People, however, still come to this spot seventy-five minutes from Birmingham and less than an hour's drive from the state capital.

Once Martin Dam was built, power surged to the area. Businesses and a lake wonderland for homesites and recreation developed.

It is difficult to pinpoint the allure of this lake, which has more than 750 miles of shoreline. Lake Martin is many things to many people—for some, a home, for others a fishing spot, a weekend getaway, a slalom course, or a romantic place to watch the sun rise and set over Alabama.

Photograph courtesy of Alabama Bureau of Tourism and Travel

Water activities are a main attraction at **Still Waters Resort** *on Lake Martin.*

Boats stand like silent sentinels guarding a marina at Still Waters Resort.

Night trolling and fishing keep some coming back. The adventurous in spirit enjoy speed or pontoon boating, skiing, knee-boarding, scuba diving, or jumping into the water from high rocks. On a typical summer weekend hundreds of boats and recreationers spill onto the lake, some on personal watercraft, others aboard motorboats or pontoons.

Temperatures in the Lake Martin area are favorable year-round, with January lows typically at 36 degrees and August highs ranging from 70 to 90 degrees. Rainfall averages about 5 inches per month, leaving plenty of sunny days to frolic at the 44,000-acre lake.

Some of the lake's most popular spots are its islands, including Chimney Rock, which juts skyward, and Acapulco Rock, where daredevils plunge from cliff ledges 75 feet above the water.

Goat Island, just north of Martin Dam, has for years been home to a herd of goats. Boaters often shimmy close along the shore, hoping to catch a glimpse. Those who come bearing food are the most likely to find a goat willing to climb down the rocky coastline to the water.

Wind Creek State Park at Lake Martin annually attracts thousands of visitors. Offering 669 campsites on some 1,400 acres, the park provides a well-rounded camping experience for a night or a month. A modern campground, Wind Creek offers spacious bathhouses and electrical, water, and sewage connections. Special services for boaters include wet storage, boat-ramp access, and plenty of fishing. Other services include picnic grounds, a sandy beach, a laundromat, a volleyball net, fishing, swimming, paddleboats, and a snack bar near the beach.

A wooden statue of the Native American maiden, **Kowaliga,** now set in a haven among the trees along the lake, had been tucked away until 1952, when Hank Williams recorded the song about a wooden Indian who fell in love with an Indian maiden at the antiques store. The maiden has left the store, but the melody lives on.

Nearby are **Church in the Pines** and **Church of the Living Waters,** both open-sided structures that offer services for worshipers who often arrive by boat. Casual attire is the norm here, where services are attended by both residents and visitors.

Like spidery fingers Lake Martin sprawls across this east-central Alabama area. Both Dadeville and Alexander City claim the wonderland. Among the sites in Alexander City is the **Sportplex,** with a war memorial, observation tower, antique fire truck, and hilltop barn.

History is only a whisper away from Lake Martin at **Horseshoe Bend National Military Park,** set on Alabama Highway 49 between New Site, Daviston, and Dadeville.

The history, fishing, boating, mild nights, and sunny days convinced one recent visitor that "Lake Martin is a little piece of paradise." Those who overheard the comment could only nod in agreement.

For more about Lake Martin call Russell Lands, 256/329-0835; Still Waters Resort and Conference Center, 888/797-3767 or 256/825-7021; Alexander City Chamber of Commerce, 256/234-3461; or Wind Creek State Park, 800/ALA-PARK (252-7275).

6 LOONEY'S TAVERN PARK AND AMPHITHEATER

THE FREE STATE OF WINSTON

An Alabama schoolteacher, long dead, has these words on his tombstone: "I love my country, my God, and my kind. I have served them all. I want no praise of song or prose."

You needed to know the man, Christopher Sheats, to truly understand these words. He lived in the era of Jefferson Davis and Robert E. Lee, but he was as politically opposite them as night and day. When the hot summer sun melts beyond the hills and the stars sparkle on Winston County in northwest Alabama, you might begin to understand Sheats' epitaph.

The meaning rings clear in performances of an outdoor Civil War drama staged each year from mid-June to mid-October near Double Springs. The two-hour musical presentation immortalizes Sheats as a man of courage and conviction. Sheats is the central figure in this story about Southerners opposed to withdrawing from the Union. The tale verifies that, contrary to popular belief, many Southerners opposed that move.

Photograph courtesy of Looney's Tavern Amphitheater and Park

A narrator raises the American flag in a final scene at Looney's Tavern.

The drama retells the story of Alabama's hill people and their struggle against the South's secession. In part because they were descendants of Andrew Jackson's men who had settled the area's hill country following the Battle of New Orleans, the people of Winston County were unwilling to fight against Old Glory.

Meeting at **Looney's Tavern**, the townspeople decided that if it was legal for states to withdraw from the Union, then they could choose to withdraw from the state. A Confederate sympathizer present delivered his now-famous line: "Winston secedes, ha! The Free State of Winston." Stopping short of doing just that, the county chose to maintain its presence in the state government.

An intense debate is a high point in a drama staged in the mountains of North Alabama.

With music, dance, and humor, the outdoor drama includes scenes in an elaborate ballroom, the state capitol, and Looney's Tavern. The amphitheater is not far from the actual site of the original tavern. Built on the slope of a wooded mountainside, the setting offers a scenic Alabama backdrop.

Visitors to Winston County find not only reminders of the tragedy of war, but also a wonderland of fun. While in the area, be sure to explore **Bankhead National Forest** and **Sipsey Wilderness** and visit **Little Natural Bridge**.

Nearby is **Looney Putt**, an 18-hole miniature golf course built around a Civil War theme. The course features such traps as Looney's Tavern, Pine Torch Church, Civil War Cannon, and other names that recall North Alabama hills and the Civil War. The course is open daily throughout the season.

Also plan a trip aboard Looney's riverboat, **The Free State Lady**, which glides through the waters of Smith Lake and Sipsey River. As the sixty-passenger boat creeps 10 miles downriver, storytellers weave tall tales, many of which are not to be believed but all of which entertain. Most of the tales focus on the unusual history of Winston County and efforts by North Alabama hill people to keep Alabama out

Photograph courtesy of Looney's Tavern Amphitheater and Park

Photograph courtesy of Looney's Tavern Amphitheater and Park

Reminders of a gentle era in Southern history are showcased at Looney's Tavern Amphitheater.

of the Civil War. A full-course meal, prepared by **Sister Sara's Kitchen,** is served aboard the boat each show night. The dinner cruise returns to port in time for the evening performance at the outdoor theater.

Don't miss a meal at Sister Sara's Kitchen in the theater complex. The buffet-style restaurant specializes in hill-country cooking of the 1860s. You'll find the likes of home-cooked vegetables, fried chicken, chicken and dumplings, fried okra, cracklin' cornbread, and peach cobbler.

The outdoor drama is presented from the second week in June through the end of August, with shows nightly on Thursday, Friday, and Saturday. Although the 1,500-seat outdoor amphitheater is rarely filled to capacity, be sure to call ahead to reserve tickets and confirm hours. During the drama season, excursion cruises run twice each afternoon on Thursday, Friday, and Saturday; reservations are needed for the cruises. The amphitheater also is used to showcase the talents of recording artists such as George Jones, The Oak Ridge Boys, Neal McCoy, and Brian White (there are usually six concerts per season). For more information or to make reservations, call 800/489-5017 or 205/489-5000.

7 MONROEVILLE
WHERE'S ATTICUS?

Monroeville doesn't have as many claims to fame as a major city, but this tiny town struts broadly at the mention of its most famous native, Pulitzer Prize–winning novelist Harper Lee.

The southwest Alabama town centers around the Monroe County Courthouse, which served as a model for the courtroom scenes in the movie based on Lee's novel *To Kill a Mockingbird*. The author fashioned much of her fictional account after the town, and she modeled the book's fictional lawyer, Atticus Finch, after her father. When you visit the courthouse and ask to see Atticus, you'll learn that you are only one of a long line of visitors who ask about the make-believe character.

A section of the courthouse today houses a **Heritage Museum**. Annually, on the first two weekends in May, the Heritage Museum presents an indoor/outdoor interactive drama of *To Kill A Mockingbird*. The action begins outside the courthouse and then moves indoors for the courtroom scene. Jurors sometimes are taken from the audience. You'll need reservations for the performance.

Not far from the city square is **Rikard's Mill**, dating to 1858. Locals say this is the state's only restored gristmill still standing on its original site and still operational. The 8½-acre site includes a covered bridge and blacksmith shop.

Fifteen minutes from Monroeville is the state's second **Masonic Lodge**, where Lafayette gave the opening dedication in 1825. Next to the lodge is the home

The courthouse centering Monroeville was made famous by native daughter Harper Lee's To Kill a Mockingbird.

Photograph by Milton Fullman

Photograph by Milton Fullman

Each spring, the people of Monroeville stage an indoor and outdoor drama depicting scenes from To Kill a Mockingbird.

where William Travis lived before heading to Texas, where he commanded the Texas patriots who died defending the Alamo.

If you love shopping for bargains, don't miss Monroeville's **Vanity Fair factory outlet**, which sells women's, children's, and men's items.

Within easy driving distance of Monroeville, Greenville is another sleepy little town with gift shops and several antiques stores worth visiting. **Confederate Park**, near the center of downtown Greenville, features statues of famous people and heroes. Drive through town to enjoy the quiet streets and picturesque homes.

If roughing it is your idea of fun, stay overnight at **Claude D. Kelley State Park**, 10 miles north of I-65 on Alabama Highway 21 at the Atmore exit. The park has a couple of cabins, some picnic areas, a 25-acre lake for fishing, swimming, paddleboats and other rentals, primitive and RV sites, and a refreshment center.

Be sure to stop briefly in Frisco City, where a city park includes an old jail moved in recent years to the site, an old post office and house, and a caboose with the lettering "Ship It On The Frisco."

In Monroeville a South Alabama Avenue marker notes the site of a house where the late author Truman Capote regularly visited relatives and then lived for several years.

Annually on the last weekend in August, **Fort Mims**, south of Monroeville, provides the setting for a reenactment of a massacre that took place there in the early 1800s. Other annual events include a **Spring Festival** held the first Saturday in April, **Heritage Days** held the last Saturday in October, and an October tribute to Truman Capote.

On the second full weekend each August, Greenville hosts a **Watermelon Jubilee**. The event is held on Watermelon Hill, a spot that locals consider "the shadiest spot in Alabama." (During late August in Alabama, this can be a very popular respite.) Guests can do more than slurp melon and spit seeds, though. At the festival you will find arts and crafts, the largest-watermelon competition, and watermelon art.

For more about Greenville and the town's bed-and-breakfasts, call the chamber of commerce, 800/959-0717.

For more about Monroeville, call the chamber of commerce, 334/743-2879.

For details about the *To Kill a Mockingbird* drama, call the Heritage Museum, 334/575-7433.

8   ALABAMA PRINCESS RIVERBOAT
CHURNING THE COOSA

The first time for anything is always the best. At least that's how it was when friends invited us to come to Gadsden to share a birthday celebration aboard the riverboat **Alabama Princess.** The boat is available for individuals, and our friends had reserved it for a Sunday afternoon celebration. After all, it's not every day someone turns fifty—friends should gather to share the despair.

Once we arrived in Gadsden, we headed to the Boardwalk on U.S. 411. In the midst of bustling traffic, the red-and-white vessel waited calmly, seeming rather out-of-place in the shadow of a large shopping mall.

The double-decked paddle wheeler, following a half century of hibernation, slipped into the waters of the Coosa River in the fall of 1992. The odyssey of the boat was made possible in part by the Gadsden–Etowah Tourism Board, which had long hoped to lure a quality riverboat operation to the area. About the time the

Photograph by Milton Fullman

Near downtown Gadsden, the Alabama Princess Riverboat plies the Coosa River on daily runs and special occasions.

tourism folks were looking for an addition to their area, the riverboat's owners, Bob and Claire Enstice, and their son, Robert, were considering relocation from Florence to more stable water with better facilities. The two desires met and wed.

Before reaching Gadsden, the vessel was lifted, loaded, towed, relaunched, and restored. With a restored main deck and a covered second deck, the boat is heated and air-conditioned, has restrooms, and offers plenty of seating.

The birthday we celebrated with friends was a fun outing, enhanced by the riverbank scenery and the wind swishing past our faces. It felt good to ply the waters. On a sunny afternoon in Gadsden, we felt like Tom Sawyer and his Becky, free to explore the world and its elements. And, besides, we weren't the ones getting a year older!

Photograph by Milton Fullman

A statue of the Native American maiden Noccalula appears to be leaping over the falls where she is said to have plunged to her death many moons ago.

The *Alabama Princess* offers narrated 90-minute sightseeing tours at 2 p.m. on Saturdays and Sundays. Snacks and soft drinks are sold aboard the vessel; visitors may not carry on food or beverages. Dinner cruises, by appointment only, run Saturday evenings from 6 to 8 p.m., spring through late fall and include a buffet and live music. The *Princess* hosts cruises during special events (reservations required). There are also Christmas dinner cruises as well as New Year's Eve and Valentine specials. After taking a riverboat cruise, you'll find plenty of other things to do in the Gadsden area.

At **Noccalula Falls Park and Campground**, a 90-foot falls is overlooked by the statue of an Indian maiden reputed to have jumped when she was not allowed to marry the man she loved. Also at the park you will find a pioneer village with more than a dozen rustic buildings, a campground open year-round, and a war memorial paying tribute to some 500 Etowah County men who died fighting in U.S. wars. The park also includes a playground, carpet golf, hiking trails, a passenger train, botanical gardens, an animal park, picnic areas, and a souvenir shop.

If you're into golf, tee off at **Silver Lakes**—part of the **Robert Trent Jones Golf Trail** that winds from north to south in the state. Sprawling on some 900 acres, the course lies between Gadsden and Anniston. A *Golf Week* magazine report has called the course "a knock-out site that may someday rival Augusta National's for beauty and charm."

Located in downtown Gadsden is the **Center for Cultural Arts**. More than a gallery or theater, this is a house of learning with changing exhibits and a children's hands-on museum called **Imagination Place**. The center includes a model railroad depicting local life in the 1940s and early 1950s, and a half-dozen scale trains travel through a miniature version of the town.

Visit Gadsden in late August to attend the "**World's Greatest Outdoor Sale**," a 450-mile stretch that begins at Noccalula Falls Park and extends northward along U.S. 127 and Lookout Mountain Parkway. You'll find antiques, crafts, music, and all kinds of treasures and junk. Be prepared to bargain!

If you're looking for good places to eat in Gadsden, you'll be surprised by what this small town has to offer. Try **The Olde Warehouse restaurant,** known for its home-cooked vegetables. Or step back a few decades at **The Grill,** where sports photos and old letter sweaters blanket the walls.

For more information about the *Alabama Princess,* call 256/549-1111. For more about the Gadsden and Etowah County area, call 256/549-0351.

9 SWAMP TOUR
CURIOSITY AND THE ALLIGATOR

At **Wildland Expeditions** you get the feeling that Captain Gene Burrell is an anachronism. Here is a man who looks more like the Humphrey Bogart character in the movie *The African Queen* than like a man of the 1990s.

Burrell has skin that is tanned and wrinkled, a testimony to his years of being outdoors. He is a man who, by his own admission, always has been curious. When he was a kid growing up in Tupelo, Mississippi, he collected varmints and reptiles, many of which he traded to the Memphis Zoo. His mother squirmed at his collection of creatures, which included snakes and flying squirrels, but the youngster's inquisitiveness could not be tamed.

While growing up Burrell spent hours with his maternal grandfather, a full-blooded Choctaw Indian who taught him the ways of nature, including trees, berries, birds, and how to track. "When I started school, I couldn't believe that all the other kids didn't know the same things," Burrell says today as the wind whips his face and he points his self-designed boat, *Gator Bait*, into the **Mobile–Tensaw delta swamp.** The swamp is one of America's most diverse wildlands and the nation's largest inland delta. Because of Burrell and his insatiable curiosity, even those who don't know an iota about nature can explore these swamplands on tours offered seven days a week.

His Native American heritage and influence quickly become obvious when this man, his gray hair grown long and pulled into a ponytail, begins to explain the tidal marshes and bayous, sloughs and osprey, the mating habits of alligators, and the hundreds of bird and fish species that make this swamp their home. Burrell loves this place and, unlike anyone you've probably ever known, is at ease in this swamp.

Why does he journey into these wilds?

"Because they tell me it can't be done," he explains, standing beside a sign that announces "The captain's word is the law."

When you take a tour of the swamp with Burrell, you wouldn't want it any other way. This man obviously knows his territory, and you'll trust his word as the law in this watery turf.

Like most other first-timers on this cruise, we had come with our own misconceptions. We'd expected mosquitoes, but there were none. We'd expected to feel threatened by alligators, but they don't—and can't—climb aboard boats. We worried about snakes dangling from trees and attacking us as we glided past.

Constrictors do climb into trees, the captain said, but not to worry. "They aren't poisonous and they only want small squirrels and birds." Since we were neither, we assumed we were safe.

Burrell's combination air-and-speed boat stretches 25 feet and holds up to twenty-two passengers. Although at times it creeps slowly through the shallow swamp, it is capable of reaching speeds of 55 miles per hour should the need arise to head home quickly. Life vests stationed beneath the passenger seats have been used only once—during a hailstorm when the passengers needed protection from the pelting.

Burrell stops frequently to point out an osprey nest built high above the ground and a Civil War barge blown here decades ago by a hurricane. As he guides the boat beneath a low bridge, he directs our attention to nests built by cliff swallows that return to these structures year after year. He pauses in front of a Southern bottomland forest to explain the ecology and growth, and he tells about the original marshmallow, a confection of sweetened paste made from the root of the mallow plant found in the marshlands.

He watches as we glide along, pausing from time to time to tell about this world that seems to fit him better than a suit and tie fit most men. He talks about man and nature and about a special alligator that lives in these waters. She is a teenager he has named "Patrice." Captain Gene has trained Patrice to swim his direction when he toots his horn and bellows her name. Wanting to show his passengers, he honks and hollers, forges ahead and honks again.

"Patrice!" he yells. The call echoes through the swamps and moss-draped trees. But no Patrice.

He heads around a bend, and we still see nothing. Then in the distance we see Patrice skimming through the swamp waters, heading toward our boat. She is a 5 1/2-foot-long alligator, as wild as any you'd find. But like Pavlov's trained dogs, she comes on command to receive a reward. In this case the prize is a couple of marshmallows. Patrice swims up, opens her wide jaws, and devours the sweet treat. If alligators can smile, I believe she did.

"Now go on back and hide," admonishes the captain. "If you don't," he warns as she turns tail and shimmers away, "someone will get you, the same way they got Pee Wee and Wet Willy."

When Patrice is gone, the captain tells of his other gator buddies that apparently were killed by poachers. "People like that," he affirms, "are the scum of the earth who take advantage and contribute nothing. All things are connected, like family. We are part of a web, and what we do to the web, we do to ourselves."

Photograph by Milton Fullman

Captain Gene Burrell takes visitors deep into South Alabama swampland.

His bandwagon aside, the captain offers passengers a hint of what nature once was like. "We carry noises with us, but here it's the way things used to be." He turns off the motor to allow the silence to blanket us.

We sit still, listening to birds and crickets. The silence is finally broken by the distant wail of a train zooming down a track installed through this delta in the 1920s.

The captain notices sweat on his passengers and makes an apology. "I can't offer air conditioning, but I can make the wind blow," he smiles, revving the engine and plowing the boat through the waters. Breezes sweep across us, and we are cooled.

As the boat grows quiet, he explains that he never intended to make a business out of his swamp tours. But he discovered that people like the swamp in all seasons, even in winter when the leaves have fallen and visibility is best.

What the tours offer, Burrell continues, is "good stress management and a chance to go where no man has gone before and where no man will take his boat. When you come again," he says as we leave, "no telling where we can go. As long as there is swampland here, I'll keep poking around and opening new areas."

Wildland Expeditions runs seven days a week, with tours usually at 10 a.m. and 2 p.m.; call to make certain though since runs are scheduled based on the weather. Trips typically run 2 to $2^1/2$ hours and cover 20 to 26 miles, depending on which route Burrell chooses. Midway on the tour the boat returns to the marina for a ten-minute break. You may want to wear sunscreen and take a cooler with a cold drink.

To get to **Chickasaw Creek Marina**, take Exit 13 off I-65 and drive 2 miles east to U.S. 43. Go south about $^1/2$ mile to the marina. Every season offers something different in the swamp. If the cold doesn't bother you, consider taking a winter trip when the leaves have fallen and visibility is best. Unless you want to take the chance of being left at the dock, call 334/460-8206 to make reservations.

Grand Oak Wildlife Park, a couple of miles from the marina, is a natural habitat zoo with animals such as deer, zebra, buffalo, and giraffe. There are several ponds, including one with alligators and another with waterfowl. Several nature trails lead visitors to the state's largest live oak tree, measuring 32 feet around and estimated to be 800 to 1,000 years old. The park grounds include a gift shop and mini-golf course. Admission is charged. For details call 334/679-5757.

If you want to see and do more while in the area, drive south to Mobile to visit the city museum and the USS *Alabama* at **Battleship Park**, or try your luck at **Mobile Greyhound Park**.

10 TALLADEGA AND THE MOTOR SPORTS HALL OF FAME

ROARING IN DIXIE

Vacant grandstand seats glare as a vanload of visitors rides a section of **Talladega Superspeedway**. As the van glides along the track—making certain not to steer too high into the steep banking—those of us inside are quiet as we imagine the deafening vroom of engines and the blast of power and speed that twice each year come to this track in East Alabama. This day as we tour, however, no crowds scream, and no flagman waves a checkered flag.

For a moment I imagine a capacity crowd filling the stands and people jumping to their feet, screaming at passing cars and clapping furiously as the checkered flag is waved. Ghosts of races past seem to linger in this speedway where dreams have been chased, shattered, and captured.

Here drivers lashed into their cars have turned left, and left, and left again, vying to finish first. With their dreams and souped-up engines, competitors come to race each spring and fall at this track 40 miles east of Birmingham.

Known as the world's fastest track, the Talladega Superspeedway is home to the National Association for Stock Car Auto Racing (NASCAR). Every year the

Photo courtesy Talladega Superspeedway

A capacity crowd looks on as drivers compete at deafening speeds at Talladega Superspeedway.

Winston Select 500 and the **DieHard 500**—the state's largest happenings—draw more than 100,000 fans each. The Winston 500 runs the first Sunday in May; the DieHard 500 in the fall.

Built in 1969 on a 2,000-acre site, the track is a year-round testing facility used by Harley-Davidson Motorcycles, tire manufacturers, and carmakers. On non-race days bus tours of the track begin at the nearby **International Motorsports Hall of Fame,** a five-building complex featuring scores of famous racing cars valued at more than $18 million.

Founded to preserve the history of motorsports on a worldwide basis and to pay tribute to those responsible for the sport's growth, the hall was the brainchild of the late Bill France Sr., NASCAR president for more than two decades. Each year visitors from all fifty states and from many foreign countries converge to see the track and hall. Three of the five buildings have enormous showrooms filled with racing vehicles in mint condition.

The Daytona Room focuses on Muscle Car Heaven with seven muscle cars encircling a Corvette. Included in this display is Richard Petty's red-and-blue STP Dodge Charger, with its career of thirty-one wins and sixteen pole positions.

The UNOCAL 76 building has an assortment of cars, displays, and a Richard Petty single-seat-car simulator that gathers crowds, especially during the summer when kids are among those touring. A popular exhibit in the UNOCAL 76 building is the Budweiser Rocket Car, a 39-foot, red-white-and-blue vehicle that looks more like a missile than a car.

It takes more than a fancy set of wheels, though, to earn a place in the International Motorsports Hall of Fame and Museum complex. Two cars, in fact, earned their way there almost through the back door. During the Winston 500 in 1983, Phil Parsons' car tangled with one driven by Darrell Waltrip. A frightening eleven-car crash resulted, sending No. 66 somersaulting through the air. Ten of the drivers, including Waltrip, escaped injury, and Parsons suffered only a minor fracture. Parsons' mangled car, on display in the museum, looks just as it did following the crash.

On a spring day in 1990 at Bristol Raceway in Tennessee, Michael Waltrip experienced what many stock-car veterans consider the worst single-car crash in the sport's history. Waltrip walked away and competed again the next day. Anyone who doubts that his survival was a miracle needs only study the photograph and the car remnants on display in the International Room.

A car linked to an emergency of another sort, the energy crisis of the early 1970s, is also on display. At first glance the Sears XDH1 experimental electric car resembles any other small automobile. This sporty white car, however, is unique. Originally made to be mass produced and sold at Sears stores, the electric car can travel more than a hundred miles before it has to be plugged in. If the energy crisis had not evaporated, this car might have gained acceptance.

Most of the cars in the museum were built with longer runs in mind, and Bill Elliott's 1985 Ford Thunderbird is no exception. Winner of the 1985 Winston 500 with an average speed of 186.288 miles per hour, it holds the world record for the fastest 500-mile stock-car race ever run. That same year this flying Thunderbird also won the Daytona 500 and Southern 500.

In spring 1992 the complex introduced a library of books, magazines, and other research materials available for public use. Also that spring the Bobby Allison Memorabilia display was unveiled. It includes the 1991 Florida Governor's Cup Award, the 1983 Winston Cup Championship trophy, racing helmets and uniforms, and a unique photograph addressed to Bobby from four U.S. presidents.

The museum also conducts an annual induction ceremony to honor the sport's heroes. Tickets to races and other events are sold in the main rotunda, which takes about one hour to visit.

Although racing and Talladega have become synonymous, the town itself is a quaint place worth a day or weekend visit. Among the most interesting places is the **Silk Stocking Historic District** south of the town square. This residential section, home to the city's early elite, retains much of its nineteenth-century appearance. The site encompasses the predominantly African-American **Talladega College** and the **Alabama Institute for the Deaf and Blind.** Many of the homes are open each year on the second weekend in April for the town's annual **pilgrimage.**

Between the historic district and downtown square is the old **L&N Depot,** which today houses the city's chamber of commerce, a good place to get brochures and directions. While parked at the old depot, walk to the nearby **Davey Allison Memorial and Talladega–Texaco Walk of Fame,** which pay tribute to the popular young race-car driver who died while attempting to land a helicopter at the superspeedway.

While you're downtown check out the specialty shops, many of which are known for their antiques. Don't miss **Farmers Trading Post general store,** where you'll find horse harnesses, cowbells, and bushel baskets filled with dried beans waiting to be scooped into brown paper bags.

If you have loads of extra time, visit **Talladega National Forest,** where the trail system falls in the southernmost extension of the Appalachian Mountains. This

210,000-acre forest is studded with hardwoods, fish-filled lakes, scenic overlooks, waterfalls, and mountain streams.

Six miles from downtown Talladega, the 115-foot-long **Waldo Covered Bridge** on Alabama Highway 77 toward Ashland sits beside a gristmill that has been converted into a charming restaurant which serves outstanding food, including steaks and blackened catfish. If you plan to stay overnight you can choose from the area chain motels and a number of delightful bed-and-breakfasts.

The International Motorsports Hall of Fame, off I-20 between Birmingham and Atlanta, is open daily except some major holidays. Admission is charged. For more information call 256/362-5002.

For information about Talladega call the area's chamber of commerce at 256/362-9075.

11 TUSCUMBIA

DRAMA, DOGS, AND DITTIES

The life of Helen Keller was remarkable enough to put Tuscumbia, the small town in North Alabama where she was born, on the map. This extraordinary child grew to influence not just a nation, but the world.

Although she was born healthy, Helen became ill at nineteen months with a fever that left her blind and deaf. Frustrated with their failing efforts to communicate with this increasingly unruly and unreachable child, Helen's parents hired twenty-year-old Anne Sullivan from the Perkins Institution for the Blind in Boston to come to their aid.

As soon as Anne arrived at Ivy Green, the Kellers' house, she began teaching words to the six-year-old. After two weeks Helen had learned ten or twenty words. But that's all they were—words. Helen had connected no meaning to them.

One morning after trying to teach the words *mug* and *milk*, Anne pumped water over Helen's hand. As the water flowed, Anne formed the letters *W A T E R* into

Photograph by Milton Fullman

In North Alabama, Helen Keller's birthplace draws crowds from across the globe.

Helen's other palm. As if a lightbulb turned on, Helen made the connection. At last a word had meaning, and Anne Sullivan was on her way to earning the nickname "The Miracle Worker," a title later used by playwright William Gibson in his play about Helen and Anne. The water pump behind the house where Helen's miracle of learning began serves as the outdoor setting each summer for this drama. With professional acting and authentic costumes and sets, the story gives glimpses of a woman who dedicated her life to improving the conditions of sensory handicapped people around the world.

The outdoor drama *The Miracle Worker* is staged on weekends from late June through July. Reservations are a must. Admission is charged.

Miss Keller's Tuscumbia home, **Ivy Green,** became a permanent shrine and was placed on the National Register of Historic Places in 1954. When you visit the house you can peek through the door of the cottage where Helen was born and where her cradle and toys remain.

In the main house you can see the upstairs bedroom shared by Helen and Anne. Downstairs is the parlor where Captain Keller, a newspaper editor, would sit and read, as well as the master bedroom and dining room.

Photograph by Milton Fullman

The log cabin where blues artist W. C. Handy was born is furnished the way it would have been when he lived there.

One downstairs room is devoted to Helen's personal mementos, including her Braille typewriter. There are also items from the making of the film *The Miracle Worker*, starring Anne Bancroft as Anne Sullivan and Patty Duke as Helen. Many original furnishings and family portraits remain in the house.

For more information about Helen Keller's birthplace, contact Ivy Green, 300 West North Commons, Tuscumbia, AL 35674; 256/383-4066.

Thousands gather in Tuscumbia each June for the **Helen Keller Festival,** a week-long event commemorating the accomplishments of the town's most famous native. The celebration includes a parade through downtown streets, stage entertainment, arts and crafts, an art auction, tours of historic sites, puppet shows, and sports events and tournaments.

While in the northwest corner of Alabama, don't miss the following sites:

The **Alabama Music Hall of Fame** was established to honor famous musicians with Alabama connections. Among the items on display in this Tuscumbia site are Elvis Presley's Sun Studios recording contract, wax figures of Nat "King" Cole and Hank Williams, outfits worn by Lionel Richie and the Commodores, and a tour bus once used by the group ALABAMA.

In nearby Florence, native son W. C. Handy is remembered at the **W. C. Handy Birthplace and Museum,** which contains what has been called "the most complete collection" of the jazz king's personal papers and artifacts. Included are Handy's trumpet, his famous piano, handwritten sheet music, old photos, and household furnishings. The log cabin that houses the collection is furnished the way it might have been when the Father of the Blues lived there. An adjacent library provides a valuable resource for African-American history and culture.

Several minutes from the Handy Museum stands the 300-foot-tall **Renaissance Tower,** which houses an aquarium, an energy display, and a restaurant overlooking TVA's Wilson Dam. The food is excellent; the view, incredible. On a clear day you can see 30 miles.

Indian Mound and Museum, also in Florence, showcases an Indian ceremonial mound plus a museum that displays fluted points and pottery dating from A.D. 1200 to A.D. 1500. The mound, which may have been either a chief's house or a ceremonial temple, was surrounded by a village and cultivated fields. Relics found nearby indicate that the Indians were skilled farmers.

Pope's Tavern, a restored stagecoach inn, is now a city-operated museum in Florence. The brick building was used as a hospital during the Civil War.

Coon Dog Cemetery lies about 25 miles southwest of Tuscumbia. In the 1930s Key Underwood buried his beloved dog on the site of his final hunt, and when he

Photograph by Milton Fullman

Scores of markers, such as this one remembering Felix, dot the Coon Dog Cemetery not far from Tuscumbia.

did, he unknowingly started a tradition. Only coon dogs are allowed in this resting place where markers make for interesting reading. Each Labor Day the cemetery is the site of a celebration including barbecue, bluegrass music, and a liar's contest where owners swap tall tales about their coon dogs.

Ivy Green sits 2 miles off the junction of U.S. 72 and U.S. 43 in Colbert County and is open daily except for some holidays. Each day's final tour begins at 4 p.m. Admission is charged.

For more information about other sites in the county, contact the Colbert County Tourism and Convention Bureau, U.S. 72 West, P.O. Box 440, Tuscumbia, AL 35674; 800/344-0783 or 256/383-0783.

12 ALABAMA VINEYARDS
BOTTLE OF WINE, FRUIT OF THE VINE

The March day was fairly cool, as it usually is that time of year in Alabama. But it wasn't raining, and the sun was doing its best to shine. Kelly Bryant had chosen that day to plant his fields for another crop of muscadines, and another season of wines.

More than a decade ago Bryant, who has spent his career as a firefighter, used plants given to him by his mother to sow several acres of muscadines. When the first fruits were a hit, he and his wife, Susan, planted other grapes. In 1985 he began commercial production of wine, and **Bryant Vineyard** was born.

Since then planting, growing, and bottling have become an annual tradition for the Bryants. Weekly during the growing and harvesting seasons they leave their Birmingham home to travel to the acreage that for years has been in the family.

When you visit the vineyard you can glimpse the fruit and then step into the basement of the nearby house to see barrels, bottles, and awards. It is here that you can sip the wines and, should you find a favorite, purchase some to take home.

The Villard Blanc, a dry white wine made from a French hybrid grape, is the couple's favorite. To discover your own favorite, stop by this place nestled in a crook formed by the Coosa River backing up to Logan Martin Lake.

Most people don't expect to find winemaking in the Bible Belt. But it happens, much to the joy of wine-lovers who are convinced there may be no better wines anywhere in the country.

Two popular grapes used in the production of Alabama wines are the muscadine and the scuppernong. The muscadine, native to the southeastern United States, is a purple grape; the scuppernong, a cultivated variety of the muscadine, is yellow-hued. The muscadine has a distinct, fruity aroma, and its sweet juice has a light taste, making it ideal for wine production.

The concept of producing Southern wine may seem innovative to some, but history shows otherwise. In fact the first wine in America came from muscadine grapes. It is also reported that the country's most popular wine once was made with scuppernongs. In 1904 some scuppernong sparkling wine from the South took top honors for its category at the Louisiana Purchase Exposition in St. Louis, chosen over wines from France, Italy, and California.

At one time Alabama farmers produced wine at an annual rate of 442,000 gallons, but Prohibition put an end to the state's wine industry in the 1920s. Then in

Tony and Martha Moirrione oversee their vineyard in Wetumpka.

1979 a native farm winery went into operation in Alabama for the first time since Prohibition. Today there are other wineries.

Braswell's Winery, open since 1984, produces thirty-four different wines from various Alabama fruits, berries, and grapes. Here you'll find wines made from almost everything, including peaches, blueberries, muscadines, and strawberries. Plus there are seven different wines made from apples. The tasting room includes a video presentation of the wine-making process. Call before going because tour days are limited. The winery, located west of Birmingham, is closed January through April.

Morrione Vineyards in Wetumpka is tucked away at the southern tip of a mountain chain. This family endeavor combines old-world procedures with new-world technology. The facility includes a tasting room and some 10 acres of vineyards. Owner Tony Morrione suggests touring in August and September when the fruit is being harvested.

Call ahead before heading to any of the vineyards because tours are usually offered only on limited days and hours. You can reach Bryant Vineyard at 256/268-2638; Braswell Vineyard at 205/648-8335; and Morrione Vineyard at 334/567-9957.

VISITING ALABAMA GHOSTS
H A I N T S   A N D   B O O G E R S

When October's crisp nights and changing leaves arrive, thoughts turn to Halloween, when the kid in us imagines ghosts hiding behind trees and spirits lurking in cellars. If you have an urge to find some of Alabama's ghosts, you should have no problem: According to some ghost watchers, the state has dozens of spirits.

Some people have reported ghostly happenings in **Smith Hall** on the campus of the **University of Alabama** in Tuscaloosa. The building, which houses the Alabama Museum of Natural History, is said to be haunted by its namesake, Eugene Allen Smith, the state's first geologist, who died in 1927. People have heard unexplainable voices and ghostly footsteps and experienced other strange happenings—enough to make many students vow never to visit the hall after dark.

The **University of Montevallo,** a picturesque campus with Georgian-style buildings south of Birmingham, also has a ghost. One of the oldest buildings, **Reynolds Hall,** dates to the mid-1800s, when the university was a boys' school. The school closed during the Civil War, when young men traded books for weapons. During the brother-against-brother war, Reynolds Hall served as an infirmary for wounded and dying soldiers.

Although history does not bear out the details, some believe that at one point during the war Wilson's Raiders stormed the infirmary and killed the patients. Some believe that the ghost that haunts Reynolds Hall is the spirit of one of the patients slaughtered by Wilson and his men.

A smoking spirit lurks in the **Archives of the Birmingham Public Library,** a place where many people go to search through the **Linn-Henley Research section** for family history. One evening when archivist Dr. Marvin Whiting was working very late, he heard the elevator move and the door open and close as though someone were coming to the department's third-floor location. Yet, like the building's guard, Whiting saw nothing. Another time a book lunged from a top shelf onto the floor. A light in the archives sometimes blinks for no apparent reason and people sometimes hear unidentifiable knocking sounds. Whiting and his coworkers often mused that the sounds were caused by the ghost of the library's late director, Fant Thornley, who had dearly loved the library—and perhaps has never left it.

In 1989, years after the elevator incident, an electrician was working in the stacks, where large bookshelves are laden with government papers and documents. The workman had his back turned when he sensed someone behind him. He turned in time to see an image that made him shudder. Later when he was shown a picture of Thornley, the workman turned white and nodded a silent "yes." The workman never returned to the archives.

A broken heart is what brings the ghost of Anne Carlisle back to **Carlisle Hall**, near Marion in Perry County. In love with a Confederate soldier, she was standing

at the top of the stairs when she learned of her sweetheart's death. Hearing the news she screamed his name and fell over the stairwell to her death. People claim to still hear her screams.

The spirit of Evelyn Carter still roams **Gaineswood** in Demopolis. Miss Carter, who died there in the mid-1800s, had wanted to be buried in Virginia. Until she could be transported there for burial, her body was stored in the home's dark and dank basement. Left too long, her spirit still lingers in the house.

John Parkman, a successful businessman whose investments turned sour, is said to haunt Selma's **Sturdivant Hall**. Parkman, once president of the

Some people believe that several ghosts lurk at the University of Montevallo.

76

Photograph by Milton Fullman

With moss-draped trees, Selma's Live Oak Cemetery can be a haunting place.

First National Bank of Selma, is said to visit regularly the house he had loved in his more prosperous days.

Students still report seeing the Red Lady who haunts **Huntingdon College's Pratt Hall** in Montgomery. The ghost, who always wears red when she roams the building, is said to be a former unhappy student who died in her dorm room.

Whether or not you believe in ghosts, you're sure to have fun looking for them in Alabama. Besides, a little imagination can go a long way to make any weekend trip lively.

For details on any of these sites, contact the Alabama Bureau of Tourism and Travel, 800/ALABAMA (252-2262).

2   ALICEVILLE

THE GERMANS ARE COMIN'

Residents of Aliceville never will forget the German prisoners of war once held in their town. A museum honoring the prisoners opened in 1995, and the wartime visitors have never been far from the townspeople's memories.

Some Aliceville old-timers still talk about a summer day in 1943 as though it were yesterday. "Germans comin' in on the Frisco!" people proclaimed as residents lined the railroad tracks along Alabama Highway 17. On that day people in this west Alabama town finally confirmed the rumors: German prisoners were coming to stay in a newly constructed prison in their town. People clustered to witness the "Nazi supermen," who were expected to arrive on the late-afternoon train.

Armed with rifles, machine guns, shotguns, and pistols, companies of American soldiers lined the stretch of highway from the railroad station to the prisoner-of-war camp. One reporter wrote that this news event "rivaled the cyclone that hit Aliceville six years before."

As the townspeople looked on, 500 members of the once-invincible Afrika Korps spilled from the train. Some were bandaged, others limped, and all had been

Photograph by Milton Fullman

On display in Aliceville is a statue created by German prisoners of war.

tanned by the North Africa sun. No sooner had the first cluster of men begun to march away than another train arrived. The scene was repeated throughout the week until more than 6,000 men—fliers, tank drivers, gunners, cooks, and mechanics—had arrived in Aliceville.

Within a week it became apparent that the words of one reporter were prophetic. "Give them two weeks, and you won't recognize the place. They are damn good soldiers." The Germans set to work to transform the prison into a temporary home. They planted grass, cultivated flower gardens, built a greenhouse, and created lawns with mosaics and elaborate statues. Each month companies of prisoners competed for a beautification award.

These were not ordinary prisoners—they were German Field Marshall Erwin Rommel's finest who had been captured during the battles that raged across the desert sands of North Africa. Among the prisoners were artists, engineers, and professors—educated men enlightened enough to make their prison stay anything but ordinary. They produced works of art, wrote and published a camp newspaper, hand-carved chess sets, painted pictures, created drawings, and built furniture. Using a homemade kiln, the Germans made bricks and constructed a small amphitheater where they presented performances, including those by the prisoners' orchestra.

Today a sturdy rock hearth and a chimney topped with initials of the prisoners who built it are all that remain of the largest of the state's World War II prison camps. (The state's other camps were in Opelika, Fort McClellan near Anniston, and Fort Rucker near Enterprise.)

Interest in the camp was renewed in the early 1990s when Aliceville hosted two reunions for former prisoners and guards. In early 1995 the city opened the nation's only German POW museum to commemorate the prisoners and their years in Alabama. Housed in what once was Aliceville's Coca-Cola bottling operation, the museum has at its entrance a German-made statue that was recovered from a swamp.

The **Aliceville Museum and Cultural Arts Center** opened with plans on the drawing board for a full-size replica of a guard tower, the inside of a barracks, and a scale model of the camp. Also planned are a children's hands-on museum, a gallery for fine arts, an exhibit focusing on the history of the Aliceville area, and a re-creation of the 1940 bottling plant.

Although Aliceville is a small town, there are several other places you should not miss.

Photograph by Milton Fullman

A cemetery near Aliceville includes the grave of George Washington's bodyguard.

Bethany Cemetery includes the well-marked gravesite of James McCrory, a Revolutionary War soldier who served as a bodyguard for George Washington.

Save time for a visit to the **Tom Bevill Visitors Center** in Pickensville, 10 miles outside Aliceville. The white-columned mansion replica incorporates features from several area homes. A sweeping staircase leads to the second floor where exhibits interpret the history of Tennessee–Tombigbee Waterway. (The network connects some 16,000 miles of inland waterways and provides a route to the Gulf of Mexico for commerce between the interior of the United States and the deepwater port of Mobile and other ports on the Gulf.)

A sprawling relief map illustrates the waterway's course through locks and dams, and a model display demonstrates the lockage process. If your timing is right you can climb to the roof level and watch a vessel pass through the lock and dam below.

Next head to the adjacent *U.S. Montgomery,* which is permanently docked beside the center. Declared a National Historic Landmark, the now-retired steam-powered stern-wheeler once kept Southern rivers navigable by removing debris that threatened river traffic. Savor your time aboard the snagboat by sitting in the heavy, wooden rocking chairs in the screened area where the crew used to rest. You can see the tiny sleeping rooms and restroom facilities as well as the boat's engine rooms, along with logs and the crew's notes.

You can fish, hike, boat, water-ski, camp, picnic, hunt, or sightsee in the 13,000 acres bordering the water that have been set aside for recreational use.

For a quick diversion before leaving the area, head to Carrollton, where a face is imprinted on a windowpane at the **Pickens County Courthouse.** This face of a frightened prisoner has been preserved since 1878, and despite scrubbings and other attempts to remove the visage, it remains.

Photograph by Milton Fullman

Ten miles outside of Aliceville, the Tom Bevill Visitors Center incorporates features from several area homes.

Aliceville, in Pickens County about 40 miles west of Tuscaloosa, has two bed-and-breakfasts, **Myrtlewood** and **WillowBrooke,** both within walking distance of downtown and the museum. Another overnight option is **Voyage Motel.** Grab a lunch of home-cooked vegetables, peach cobbler, and the fried chicken or catfish at **The Plantation House,** a building completed in 1905 and moved to its present site in the mid-1980s. The house, once the home of the owner of a lumber company and sawmill, is on the Alabama Register of Historic Landmarks.

For more information about the Aliceville area and POW museum, contact the city's chamber of commerce at 205/373-2820 or the museum at 205/373-2363.

3 AVE MARIA GROTTO
THE WORKS OF ONE MONK

In the northern Alabama town of Cullman you will find evidence of what a single, dedicated man can accomplish. Ave Maria Grotto is the work of a monk who spent his lifetime mixing "junk" with concrete to create miniature memorials of some of the world's great shrines, architectural marvels, and religious events. There is something intriguing about a man who could take old objects like glass, beads, taillights, and perfume bottles, and make something spectacular.

Ave Maria Grotto, a 4-acre park, is on the grounds of St. Bernard Abbey, the first and only Benedictine monastery in Alabama. In the German-rooted city of Cullman, the abbey is home to a few dozen monks.

A 2-block-long wooded pathway leads to the shrine, which includes 125 miniature structures of world-famous sites. These replicas, ranging in height from 3 inches to 6 feet, are the work of Brother Joseph Zoettl. In 1918 Brother Joseph, a tiny workaholic of a monk, was put in charge of a power plant that furnished heat to St. Bernard Abbey. Born in Bavaria as Michael Zoettl, the bored "Brother Joe" began to make small shrines in the basement of the power station. Those first creations, formed from pumice, concrete, and clinkers from the power station's boilers, were intended only for the other monks.

The monk made several thousand small religious objects before hitting on the idea of erecting something permanent. In time what began as an amusement became a life's work. As

Photograph by Milton Fullman

Miniatures of renowned world sites are clustered at Ave Maria Grotto in Cullman.

word spread about what Brother Joseph had created, more and more visitors came, and the grotto was moved from the abbey's gardens to its present location in an old rock quarry.

Brother Joseph's first creation became The Main Grotto, a place intended for prayer and meditation. Once that taproot was in place, the busy monk spent most of his time in the quarry, landscaping to add the miniatures he had assembled in the 5-foot-square basement workroom. Throughout both World War II and the Korean War the shy little man labored. Failing in health in 1958, Zoettl, at age eighty, began to fashion his final major piece, a miniature of the basilica of Lourdes. Three years later Brother Joseph died, leaving behind a mon-

Photograph by Milton Fullman

At Ave Maria grotto, a visitor notes Brother Joseph's attention to detail.

ument to man's ingeniousness and patience. Brother Joseph is buried in **Monastic Cemetery,** only a stroll away from the grotto along a tranquil lane lined by the Stations of the Cross.

Brother Joseph, who rarely traveled, used postcards, pictures, and what he had learned through his reading to create objects that continue to fascinate visitors. His works, nestled along a shaded hillside, are miniatures of the Temple of Jerusalem, St. Peter's Shrine, Noah's Ark, the Hanging Gardens of Babylon, the Pantheon, the Roman Colosseum, the Leaning Tower of Pisa, and more than a hundred others.

While in **Cullman,** pay a visit to the town itself. Settled in 1873 by German immigrant John Cullman, this city midway between Huntsville and Birmingham has three shopping centers, several department stores, an amateur theater, walking trails, two golf courses, and a downtown museum with artifacts from the city's founder.

Southwest of Cullman, fishermen have pulled world-record spotted bass from Smith Lake's acres of clear water. **Smith Lake Park** offers carpet golf, a waterslide, a swimming pool, camping facilities, boat slips and launch ramps, and picnic pavilions.

Sportsman's Lake, north of Cullman off U.S. 31, offers fishing, picnicking, camping, carpet golf, a playground, and paddleboats.

Annual events in Cullman include a **Bluegrass Festival,** a summertime bass classic, and a fall county fair. Take advantage of the huge flea market open on weekends at the Cullman exit off I-65.

About 50 miles north of Birmingham and 4 miles off I-65, Ave Maria Grotto is open daily except Christmas from 7 a.m. until sunset. Admission is charged.

For more information about Cullman, call the Cullman Area Chamber of Commerce at 256/734-0454.

For more about Ave Maria Grotto, contact St. Bernard Abbey, 1600 St. Bernard Drive Southeast, Cullman, AL 35055; 256/734-4110.

4 BELLINGRATH GARDENS IN THEODORE
A PROMISE TO HIS MAMA

Never mind that the days have turned cool and that most of our lawns and gardens are looking ragged. Flowers know no season at this Alabama haven.

Bellingrath Gardens, about 20 miles south of Mobile in Theodore, consists of 65 landscaped acres nestled in a 905-acre semitropical forest. The grounds are filled with flowers, trees, and birds. And, thanks to their southern exposure, the gardens bloom year-round.

The gardens were the brainchild of Walter Bellingrath, who helped introduce Coca-Cola to a thirsty South. In 1918, after Walter and Bessie Bellingrath bought the land, Bessie set about transforming the woodland into gardens. The Bellingraths opened their gardens to the public in 1932. Five years later the couple built a home in the heart of the formal gardens and furnished the house with fine antique furniture, Oriental rugs, silver, china, and what today is considered the world's largest public display of Boehm porcelain.

The collection includes some 230 pieces of Edward Marshall Boehm's hard-paste porcelain. It contains a sampling of Boehm's art, from the religious figurines he first sculpted, through the period he created animals, and finally to his favorite subjects, birds and flora. The display is centered around the largest piece of porcelain Boehm ever attempted, the Ivory Billed Woodpecker.

Bellingrath once promised his mother that he intended "to make the world better and brighter by my being here." His promise has been recognized by thousands, including American Garden Guidebook, which has called Bellingrath Gardens "Perhaps the most beautiful garden in the southeastern United States and one of America's top five."

Part of the beauty is that something is always blooming in Bellingrath. Camellias begin to bloom as early as September and continue to

Photograph courtesy of Bellingrath Gardens

At Bellingrath Gardens, the Southern Belle daily takes visitors on excursions on the Fowl River.

flower until mid-April, with many of the rarest and finest varieties in full bloom before and during Christmas.

Roses generally come into bloom here the first week of May and extend into November. During November, the peak season for chrysanthemums, tens of thousands of blooms drape the iron lacework balconies of the fifteen-room Bellingrath home. Known as **Bellingrath Gardens' Chrysanthemum Extravaganza,** the fall showing features garden mums, graceful cascade varieties in large baskets, and stately monoliths. These fall blooms of yellow, bronze, lavender, wine, and white make up one of the world's largest outdoor displays of mums presented as topiary columns, standards, baskets, butterflies, and peacocks.

Exquisite camellias line garden paths from September to early February, with blooms too plentiful to count. The well-tended gardens teem with flowering shrubs: crape myrtle, gardenia, hydrangea, dogwood, wisteria, and Confederate jasmine. And the fragrances of hemerocallis, azaleas, and sweet or tea olive fill the gardens September through May.

In December you will see floods of poinsettias, flowering cabbage kale, camellias, and pansies. Don't miss the poinsettia Christmas tree renowned for its beauty and design. Christmas week features hot cider and cookies served in the Bellingrath home, which is decorated to the hilt for the holiday season.

More than seventy varieties of native trees, sculptures, reflecting pools, and waterfowl grace the gardens. Winding paths, wrought-iron bridges, waterfalls, lily pads, and singing birds complement this serene spot.

From a distance, the intricate setting of each garden looks like part of a needle-point creation. After visiting this South Alabama site, you'll agree that Walter made good on his promise to Mama.

The gardens and house are open daily; hours vary according to the season. Plan to spend at least ninety minutes touring the gardens, and add another hour to tour the home. You can also take a cruise aboard the ***Southern Belle.*** Admission is charged. The best price includes the cruise plus admissions to the house and gardens. If you need other weekend ideas, head to Mobile, where the possibilities are endless.

For more information about Bellingrath call 334/973-2217.

5   BIRMINGHAM
BROWSING IN THE MAGIC CITY

D espite national misconceptions Birmingham is much more than steel mills and racial strife. It is a complex town, very unlike its national image.

Begin exploring the state's largest city by visiting the **Alabama Sports Hall of Fame,** which showcases legendary native Alabama sports personalities. Notable moments from sports fill wall cases and floor displays, and you'll be captivated whether you're an athlete, fan, or admirer of some of the nation's best. You'll see the hat of a famous coach, the trophy of a great quarterback, and uniforms from major league teams of the 1920s and '30s. Your tour will begin with a brief film heralding the collection, which takes one to two hours to absorb.

Also in downtown Birmingham you'll find the **Museum of Art,** where you can grab a quick lunch at the **Terrace Cafe** overlooking the museum's outdoor sculpture garden. The museum is the Southeast's largest municipal museum.

Another downtown must-see is **Linn Park,** which anchors the northern end of **Birmingham Green.** Surrounded by the Jefferson County Courthouse, Birmingham City Hall, the original section of the Birmingham Public Library, and Boutwell Auditorium, the park often provides the setting for art shows, concerts, music, and midday breaks. The year's most major event held here is **City Stages,** a three-day music fest each June.

Near the Birmingham airport you'll find the **Southern Museum of Flight,** displaying aircraft, models, photographs, and memorabilia, most of which detail early aviation and the heroic exploits of the world's original frequent fliers. Among the exhibits you will see a 1925 crop duster, a 1910 Curtis "Pusher," and an F-4 Phantom jet.

Be sure to save time for the **Barber Vintage Motorsports Museum,** which displays some of the world's rarest

Photograph by Milton Fullman

Now idle, the furnaces at Sloss have become permanent reminders of the city's roots.

Photograph by Milton Fullman

Birmingham's most noted landmark, Vulcan, oversees downtown Birmingham.

motorcycles—from 1960s British Triumphs to Italian Ducatis.

At **Sloss Furnaces,** on the edge of downtown Birmingham, the preserved blast furnaces serve as a constant reminder of the iron industry that gave birth to Birmingham. For nearly ninety years this facility produced pig iron for the city's foundries and mills.

Begin your exploration of the areas south of the city at **Vulcan,** the world's largest iron statue and the second largest U.S. statue, taking backseat only to the Statue of Liberty. Cast from 100 percent Birmingham iron ore, Vulcan was created as the city's exhibit for the 1904 St. Louis World's Fair. Standing atop Red Mountain, this "god of the forge" overlooks the Magic City.

South of downtown you'll find **Birmingham Zoo,** one of the Southeast's largest with a hundred acres of parkland and hundreds of animals. One of the state's most visited sites, the zoo has a mini-train, gift shop, snack bar, and picnic tables.

At the **Birmingham Botanical Gardens,** across the street from the zoo, you'll see flora from around the world and the Southeast's largest climate-controlled conservatory. The Japanese Gardens offer an Oriental setting that includes a teahouse.

West of the city you'll find **Arlington Antebellum Home and Gardens.** The two-story, Greek Revival mansion is the area's only remaining antebellum home. Unlike the other pre-Civil War homes that were destroyed, this one survived because it was used as headquarters for Union officers. The restored home is outfitted with period antiques and decorative arts.

Be sure to visit **Irondale Cafe** on the east side of downtown. This cafeteria inspired actress Fannie Flagg's successful novel *Fried Green Tomatoes at the Whistle Stop Cafe,* which was made into a popular movie.

If you want to stay overnight in downtown Birmingham, you have several excellent options, including the historic **Redmont Hotel,** the **Tutwiler Hotel,** and the **Sheraton Civic Center Hotel.**

Birmingham's newest attractions also offer a host of fun. **VisionLand,** Alabama's family theme park, provides thrill rides and attractions for all ages. The park includes a water park, a sprawling family arcade, a giant wooden roller coaster, restaurants, and an entertainment center with an in-line skating rink, bowling alley, and fourteen-screen theater.

McWane Center: Adventures in Science, in the renovated Loveman's building at the heart of downtown, includes an **IMAX dome theater,** an ocean pool, World of Water exhibits, a collection of interactive science exhibits, and a simulated space-flight experience.

For more information about the city and its attractions, call the Greater Birmingham Convention and Visitors Bureau at 800/458-8085 or 205/458-8000.

Photograph by Milton Fullman

Arlington is Birmingham's only remaining antebellum home.

6 BLOUNT COUNTY
COVERED BRIDGES

As I stared at the majestic bridge, its trusses and ties, its foundation and graffiti, I asked a question that I later learned every first-timer poses: "Can we really use it?"

The wood and its craftsmanship hint at the bridge's age, like wrinkles on a woman's aging face. But like the stamina of a matriarch whose strength belies her years, the bridge's foundation, I was told, is sturdy.

Here in Blount County, a North Alabama region that has earned a reputation as the "Covered Bridge Capital of Alabama," stand three of the state's remaining twelve covered bridges. All are within a few miles of Oneonta.

In answer to my question I learned that the bridges are still serviceable, robust enough to hold up to three tons, and strong enough to allow passage to visitors.

Blount County's bridges, all three of which are on the National Register of Historic Places, have been extensively renovated through the years. Their foundations and primary structures are original, preserved by the roofs that were, from the beginning, intended to protect the untreated wood from weathering. Wooden shields along the sides kept horses from being frightened by seeing the water below. As the bridges are only one-lane wide, drivers in approaching cars must pause to see whether another driver is coming from the opposite direction.

Since 1967, Alabama has lost ten of its covered bridges, leaving survivors in Blount, Sumter, Calhoun, Cullman, Etowah, Talladega, Coosa, and Lee Counties.

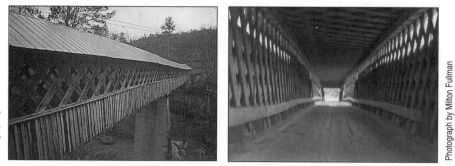

Photograph by Milton Fullman

Photograph by Milton Fullman

The bridges of Blount County are a photographer's delight.

Blount County had four bridges until 1993, when vandals burned the county's longest covered bridge, the Nectar Bridge, which stretched 385 feet.

It was not the area's first loss. As recently as the 1960s the county had sixteen covered bridges; but progress and plans called for their replacement by modern structures until someone pointed out that history was being destroyed with each plank that was removed. The destruction halted.

The 220-foot-long **Horton Mill Bridge**, the country's highest covered bridge above water, is a couple of miles north of town and a favorite spot for photographers.

Swann Bridge, near Cleveland about 10 miles from Oneonta, is

A meditation chapel in Palisades Park has a view of the Appalachian foothills.

Alabama's longest bridge, spanning 324 feet across the Locust Fork of the Black Warrior River. The longest remaining covered bridge in the county, Swann Bridge was built in 1933.

Easley Bridge, 3 miles northwest of Oneonta, is only 95 feet across. It was built in 1927, making it one of the state's oldest covered bridges.

Although the bridges are the reason that many visit here, there is plenty more in Blount County to keep folks busy.

Palisades Park, a nationally acclaimed multi-use park, offers nature trails and a meeting center. Located 5 miles northwest of Oneonta, off U.S. 231, this 90-acre park has shaded picnic areas and a playground.

From here you can get a spectacular view of the countryside and Appalachian foothills as they ripple into Blount County. Pioneer buildings that have been moved to the site include log cabins, a barn, corncrib, meditation chapel, one-room schoolhouse, and a small museum displaying period farm items. Some people come here to rappel the cliffs.

Blount County Memorial Museum in Oneonta's Courthouse Square displays arrowheads, sandstone, covered-bridge art, maps, and a Thomas Edison collection. It is open limited hours.

Not far from Oneonta you'll find **Rickwood Caverns State Park**. With a mile of underground caverns, this is the only caving park in the state park system. The subterranean mile is composed of passages and lighted rooms accented with thousands of sparkling white, limestone formations. These caverns were water-formed more than 260 million years ago. Water droplets constantly drip from the stalactites and slide down the stalagmites, making this a still-active living formation.

Off I-65 in southwest Blount County, Rickwood Caverns State Park includes picnic areas, campgrounds, carpet golf, a miniature train, game machines, a snack bar, hiking trails, a playground, and a swimming pool. There is a charge for cave admission, swimming, and camping. Cave tours are available 7 days a week Memorial Day through Labor Day, and on weekends during some other months.

Circle M Feed and Western, on Alabama Highway 79 near Oneonta, makes a fun stop-off. Here you'll find Western wear and boots for sale and a curious collection of animals that includes llamas, pigmy goats, emus, fainting goats, camel, reindeer, miniature horses, and potbellied pigs. You can't miss this store—it's topped with a gigantic boot that must stand 5 or 6 feet tall. If you know an infant cowhand, this is the place to shop—boots come as tiny as size zero.

Water sports play a main role in recreation in this area. Just minutes from Oneonta, off U.S. Highway 231, is the 500-acre **Highland Lake,** which offers public boat ramps, plus boating and swimming facilities.

The Locust and Mulberry forks of the Black Warrior River provide opportunities for canoeing and kayaking. Both waterways wind through the county, offering lazy drifts and whitewater action.

Most anything you can think of to do on water can be done at the 1,095-acre **Inland Lake.** This stocked, scenic lake provides ample opportunity for fishing and fun.

To showcase its most famous features, Blount County annually hosts a **Covered Bridge Festival** on the fourth weekend in October, the same time the leaves turn red, orange, and yellow. The festival includes bridge tours, arts and crafts, a tennis tournament, a quilt show, and a ByGone Days celebration in Palisades Park. You can venture on your own during the Covered Bridge Festival or take a bus tour; be sure to make reservations ahead of time for the bus tour. Windwood Inn (800/233-0841) offers choice accommodations.

A memorable experience awaits you at **Capps Cove Bed and Breakfast**. You can stay overnight in one of two bedrooms at Sybil and Cason Capps's sprawling, two-story home or in one of the their two log cabins. The cabins, which look rustic, have microwaves, stoves, modern baths, fireplaces, a few munchies, and front porches with rockers and views of the property's stream and wooded acreage. The Capps serve an elaborate breakfast in the main house. Call 800/583-4750 for more information.

For more information about other sites in North Alabama, contact the Alabama Mountain Lakes Association, 800/648-5381 or 256/350-3500.

For details about Oneonta, its covered bridges, and other local attractions, contact the Blount County–Oneonta Chamber of Commerce, 227 Second Avenue East, P.O. Box 87, Oneonta, AL 35121; 205/274-2153.

Photograph by Milton Fullman

Two rustic-looking but modern cabins at Capps Cove, above and right, include all the comforts of home, plus a cozy fire in winter.

7 TUSCALOOSA
TOUCHDOWN!

On fall weekends you will see and hear the words "Roll Tide" and "Alabama Crimson Tide" everywhere at the **University of Alabama.** Worn on the clothes of loyal fans, the messages leave no doubt about these folks' allegiance.

The football tradition runs deep in Tuscaloosa, where the Tide spirit reaches its peak during the fall when the team battles opponents on its home turf.

Many colleges have football, but few take their game as seriously as do fans of the Crimson Tide. On game days reds and whites are everywhere—on people's bodies, on banners stretched across streets, and on fraternity and sorority houses.

Fans paint Crimson Tide symbols on their faces or write with shoe polish on their cars and trucks. Some fans tote empty boxes of Tide detergent and rolls of toilet tissue to symbolize the team's go-for-victory chant, "Roll Tide." (Any team caught in the wake of that roll knows how powerful a punch it can pack.)

This town, the school, its students, its alumni, and its friends are serious about Alabama football. So intense are they that in the late 1980s the university opened a museum that displays more than a century of football glory, focusing on the sport, its players, its impact, and the coaches who molded the tradition.

The museum is named for the Tide's legendary coach, Paul W. "Bear" Bryant, three-time winner of the National

Photograph by Milton Fullman

The legacy of the University of Alabama's athletic history is remembered at the Paul W. Bryant Museum.

Coach of the Year, eight times named Southeastern Conference Coach of the Year, and the first coach since the formation of the NCAA to win a hundred games in one decade.

The museum's collection, set in the shadow of the stadium where home games are played, centers on football. You'll see photographs, uniforms, programs, videos, and sports memorabilia dating from 1892. The museum also has films, correspondence, documents, memorabilia, and publications pertaining to Southeastern Conference sports.

The university's football teams have created some heart-stopping moments of play and captured a dozen national championships from 1892 to 1992. The museum preserves many of these times.

You will begin your visit by viewing The Bryant Legacy, a short film that traces Bryant's life, career, and philosophy. Next you will enter a simulation of Coach Bryant's office as he left it in 1983. There you will see the coach's trademark hound-stooth hat and field jacket.

Museum-goers join the excitement of a game-day crowd and go behind the scenes with the computer-controlled, touch-screen video "Echoes of Heroes," a tribute to the game's other heroes: the band, cheerleaders, staff, and fans. A video library, with films dating to the 1920s that have been transferred from 16-milli-meter film to videotape, documents the history of Alabama football.

On game days the museum overflows with fans getting into the spirit before the gridiron clash or reveling in the atmosphere after a duel. Other days, when the fans and their "Roll Tide" T-shirts have headed home, are less crowded.

Paul W. Bryant Museum, on the University of Alabama campus, is open daily. Admission is charged. For more information call 205/348-4668.

While you're on the university campus be sure to visit the **Gorgas House.** Built in 1892 as a dining hall the house was later associated with the Gorgas family, whose son helped to eradicate the yellow-fever epidemic, thus paving the way for completion of the Panama Canal.

Also on campus you will find the **Alabama Museum of Natural History,** which exhibits portions of state geologic formations and fossils in re-created natural habitats.

While in Tuscaloosa don't miss the **Children's Hands-On Museum;** **Old Tavern,** once a stagecoach stop, a residence, and an inn; **Capitol Park,** former site of the state capitol when Tuscaloosa was the seat of government; **Battle–Friedman House,** an early 1800s mansion open for tours; and the **Mildred Warner Home,** which is filled with fine art, antiques, and historic architecture.

In 1997 Mercedes-Benz opened its first American manufacturing plant in Vance, midway between Tuscaloosa and Birmingham, where it produces the popular ML320 sport-utility vehicles. (Americans got their first look at the new Mercedes M-Class in Steven Spielberg's thriller *The Lost World*.) The Mercedes site includes a visitors center and museum that features the company's past and present. Displays include video presentations, interactive modules, and actual vehicles from the Mercedes collection. You can tour the factory and buy Mercedes merchandise and collectibles in the gift shop.

Admission price at the **Mercedes Visitors Center and Museum** includes factory tours when space is available. For reservations call 888/286-8762.

For more information about Tuscaloosa contact the city's Convention and Visitors Bureau at 800/53T-TOWN (8-8696).

Photograph by Milton Fullman

The Mercedes Visitors Center showcases both old and new Mercedes-Benz vehicles.

8 DOTHAN
DOING THE PEANUT CAPITAL
OF THE WORLD

The old chair sits undisturbed on the second floor of **Porter Hardware**, where sun streams through a smudgy window as the world passes by below on downtown Dothan's main thoroughfare. For years the chair has sat that way, as though awaiting its owner's return.

The owner of this chair has been dead since 1944, but several of the men who work here still remember E. R. Porter who, with J. D. Murphree, opened the store in 1889. To sit in his chair or to adopt it for their own use would somehow be a sacrilege.

"That's Mr. Porter's chair," explains Milton Arnold, who began working at Alabama's oldest continuously operating hardware store before Porter's death. "The

Photograph by Milton Fullman

Photograph by Milton Fullman

(Left) Dating to 1889, Porter Hardware still is serving customers.
(Right) Murals on downtown Dothan buildings depict the region's history.

Photograph by Milton Fullman

A gold peanut stands outside the Dothan Visitors Center.

world has changed and so has hardware," says Arnold, now a man with gray hair who gets about this store with a spryness that belies his years.

Things may have changed beyond these walls, but little evidence of the passing of time exists inside this store, which still contains rolling ladders, wood-and-glass display cases, and wood floors scarred and scuffed like soldiers returning from battle.

The business, which serves customers from the three states whose boundaries meet near this southeast corner of Alabama, is within walking distance of several other must-see sites in downtown Dothan.

Murals painted by world-renowned artists on the sides of downtown buildings detail the history of the region. You will find it difficult to pass these sprawling works of art without stopping to ponder the origin and roots of this chiefly agricultural city.

The nearby **Wiregrass Museum of Art** features changing exhibits of art from the nineteenth and twentieth centuries. Youngsters will especially enjoy the hands-on exhibits on the second level.

The 1915 **Dothan Opera House,** adjacent to the civic center, is an impressive neoclassical-revival structure which hosts regular performances. Be sure to call in advance to arrange a tour.

Up the street from the civic center you'll find **Cherry Street A.M.E. Church,** originally organized in 1877 as the Colored Methodist Church. The state's oldest A.M.E. church, it has been declared the "Mother Church" of Alabama's A.M.E. denomination. You can call ahead to schedule a tour or just visit the 1908 building on your own.

Stop at the **Dothan Area Convention and Visitors Bureau,** 3311 Ross Clark Circle at the corner of Choctaw Street, to collect information for your visit. The center is near **Water World,** the area's only wave pool, which includes a 400-foot waterslide, video arcade, and children's play area.

Be sure to snap a picture of your group alongside the gold statue of a peanut outside the visitors center, which is what put this place on the map. Known as the Peanut Capital of America, Dothan annually hosts the **National Peanut Festival,** two weeks of festivities that include national celebrities, a carnival, fair, parade, beauty pageant, and peanut-recipe contest. The events begin on the first Friday in November.

"Call Dothan the heart of Southern hospitality," says Lin Graham, director of the city's visitors bureau in this region where the stiff, dry grass has given rise to the area's nickname, the Wiregrass. Today Dothan plays down its peanut involvement because too many tourists, no matter what month they visit, are disappointed if they don't see peanuts being harvested. Peanuts, too, have their season.

One of the best places to observe the other Southern nut, the pecan, is **Troy Simms Pecan Company.** During peak season, which is November through December, you can see farmers bring their crops to sell at Simms. As you look on, the pecans are cracked, graded, and then sold.

While you're in town don't miss Dothan's two dinner theater groups, **"Grits on the Side"** and **"The Opus Nostrum Touring Company."**

If you want a guaranteed good meal, stop by **Garland House** for lunch. In a renovated 1914 house 2 blocks from downtown on North Bell Street, Garland House serves only weekday lunches. For authentic Italian food prepared by Chef T. J. Mitchell, visit **Paparazzi** on U.S. 231 South. And if hunger strikes while you're downtown, try **Poplar Head Mule Company and Grill,** a one-time mule buggy store in the central business district.

Other Dothan-area activities include golf at **Highlands Oaks** on the Robert Trent Jones-designed course and shopping in one of the area malls or antiques stores.

Dothan is blessed with plenty of quality hotels and motels. One of the best is **Comfort Inn** on Ross Clark Circle.

For more about the city, call the Dothan Area Convention and Visitors Bureau, 334/794-6622. If the lives of the area's early settlers intrigue you, head 3 miles north of Dothan on U.S. 431 to **Landmark Park.** Here you'll find a farm museum where the beds are a bit ruffled, an apron hangs in the kitchen, and a shaving mug and brush wait on a washstand. It seems as though the farm family might soon be back. In the meantime you can poke about a bit to see how the farm operated, check on the sheep and goats, and look at the smokehouse, cane mill, and syrup shed.

In addition to the clapboard farmhouse, you can tour a turn-of-the-century church, a Victorian gazebo, a one-room schoolhouse, a country store, interpretive center, planetarium, and an 1,800-foot boardwalk that offers the chance to spot beavers, possums, foxes, and turtles. A level boardwalk makes the trek easy enough even for those not in the best of shape. Pavilions and benches along the way offer respite.

Photograph by Milton Fullman

A monument in downtown Enterprise pays tribute to the boll weevil.

Pack a picnic and plan to spend several hours at Landmark Park. You can spread your outdoor feast on one of the tree-shaded tables adjacent to the interpretive center. Each fall Landmark Park hosts **Pioneer Peanut Days** and a **Fall Folklife Festival.**

When you are ready to leave "yesterday" behind at Landmark Park, step into "today" at **Farley Nuclear Visitors Center,** 20 miles east of

Dothan. Films trace the history of energy from prehistoric times to nuclear generators. Children especially enjoy the hands-on displays and a chance to converse with a walking, talking robot. Call ahead for more information about robot shows.

Another must-see is the **U.S. Army Aviation Museum at Fort Rucker,** west of Dothan and just north of Enterprise. On this training base for military helicopter pilots, the museum details the history of U.S. Army aviation with one of the world's largest collections of helicopters, including the first helicopter and the AH-74 Apache, hero of Desert Storm. Exhibits include life-size dioramas, films, and interpretive material.

A farmhouse at Landmark Park helps a new generation understand the past.

Photograph by Milton Fullman

While you're in Enterprise, drive by the **Boll Weevil Monument,** the nation's only memorial to an insect! It honors the insect that devoured the area's cotton crops and compelled farmers to diversify, which led to their successful venture into raising peanuts.

9 EUFAULA

OLD HOUSES AND HISTORY

When I'm asked where to find some of Alabama's most charming old homes, my mind flies to Eufaula. Charming, quiet, and slow-paced, this town saddles up to the Georgia border on Alabama's east boundary. Here residents have preserved their homes, celebrated their heritage, and savored their nature wonderland.

Each April the city hosts a three-day pilgrimage, offering visitors a chance to peek inside their doors.

For those who can't coordinate their visit with the pilgrimage, the columned **Shorter Mansion** is open year-round. This neoclassical-revival mansion, extensively remodeled in 1906, houses the **Eufaula Historical Museum** and **Eufaula Heritage Association.**

Fendall Hall, an Italianate-style home once used as a hospital for Confederate wounded, is now a city museum.

Photograph by Milton Fullman

In Eufaula, Shorter Mansion is open year-round for tours.

Eufaula's **Seth Lore and Irwinton Historic District,** with more than 700 historic and architecturally significant structures, includes Alabama's most coherent collection of intact mid- to late-nineteenth century small-town commercial buildings.

Although seeing old homes is a constant lure to this charming town along the Chattahoochee Trace, there are plenty of other things you can do year-round in Eufaula.

Lakepoint State Park Resort, 7 miles north of Eufaula, provides a wonderful family vacation spot. Stretching along the 45,000-acre Lake Eufaula, which has been called the largemouth bass capital of the world, Lakepoint is more than a fisherman's paradise.

The resort includes a 101-room lodge; hiking trails winding through pine woods; picnic area with pavilions, tables, grills, and a playground; a quarter-mile beach with bathhouse; lighted tennis courts; and a swimming pool. There are also heated and air-conditioned cabins, many with fireplaces. A 244-site campground offers water and electric hookups, plus a community center, beach, boat ramp, bathhouse, laundry facilities, and a camp store.

Part of the fun at Lakepoint is watching the fish weigh-ins at the marina. And you can rent both a boat and a guide to go after your own catch. According to those who hunt and fish in the area, it is possible to take an 8-point buck and an 8-pound bass in the same day at Lake Eufaula.

The community has one elegant bed-and-breakfast, **Kendall Manor Inn,** and there may be no better way to step back into the nineteenth century than to snuggle into a four-poster bed, disappear in the down comforter, and wake to the aroma of breakfast being prepared. Completed in 1872, Kendall Manor Inn is filled with exquisite detail and, according to some, a ghost who occasionally makes himself known.

About 4 miles north of Eufaula, more adventure awaits at **Tom Mann's Fish World,** a noted aquarium complex where you can view largemouth bass and other species.

If you don't want to step too far back into time for fear of losing sight of places to tee off, be sure to visit **Red Eagle Golf Course**, a semi-private course where several holes overlook Lake Eufaula. You can also play a round at the course at Lakepoint State Park Resort.

Eufaula National Wildlife Refuge, adjacent to Lakepoint State Park, is farmed during the growing season and flooded during the migratory season to provide a resting place for migratory birds. A federal preserve for protection of waterfowl and wild game, the refuge offers hiking trails, observation towers,

Photograph by Milton Fullman

Kendall Manor Inn, dating to 1872, today is a bed-and-breakfast.

and scenic driving tours. It is open during daylight hours for wildlife-oriented, recreational activities such as seasonal fishing and hunting. You can boat, hike, and observe wildlife in authorized areas.

Be sure not to overlook the nation's first **Vietnam Memorial.** You will find it on North Eufaula Avenue across from Shorter Mansion.

Eufaula hosts the **Indian Summer Arts and Crafts Festival** every fall. Celebrating the city's Indian heritage and mild fall weather, the festival is held in the Seth Lore Historic District and offers live entertainment, spin art, clothesline art, and hands-on crafts, plus a midway of foods, children's games, and activities.

For more information about Eufaula, call the city's tourism council at 800/524-7529. For more information about the surrounding area, call the Historic Chattahoochee Commission, 334/687-9755.

A visit to Eufaula would not be complete without a taste or two of Lake Eufaula Punch. Just remember that, according to those who know the power of its punch, there is a two-cup limit. If you want to make this powerful punch yourself, here's the secret recipe from the folks in Eufaula.

LAKE EUFAULA PUNCH

Juice from one dozen lemons (save the rinds)
1 cup honey
One fifth of gin

Thoroughly mix lemon juice and honey. Add gin and lemon rinds. Let mixture sit overnight in a crock. (Leave the lemon rinds in the punch while it ages.)

Next morning, lift out the rinds and squeeze them again. Strain the punch before serving it in old-fashioned glasses over finely crushed ice.

10   MOBILE BAY
TWO FORTS AND A FERRY

The sun had not been long in the sky the morning my husband, Milton, and I arrived at **Fort Morgan,** 22 miles west of Gulf Shores. Dew blanketed the grass and clouds filled the sky as we forged ahead. We knew that this was not the smartest way to visit, but we preferred to discover this historic site without the benefit of a guide. That way we could pretend to discover it ourselves.

We entered a tunnel through a wall of a fortified kingdom—a fort that once protected the region from intruders arriving by water. Fort Morgan was first used by the Spanish in the 1500s. U.S. troops built the present structure during the early 1800s for protection against Native Americans. But it was during the Civil War that the fort became a pivotal setting.

Without outlining a plan, Milton and I passed through the tunnel and headed in opposite directions. I turned left, losing myself beneath vaulted arches inside dark,

Fort Morgan, along Mobile Bay, has played a key role in Alabama history.

dank, dungeonlike rooms. As I pondered what life must have been like for the soldiers once stationed here, a bird that I disturbed scampered nearby. Unnerved, I stepped outside to the grassy enclosure and looked around for Milton, the only other person here on this quiet morning.

Milton meanwhile had trekked up steep stone steps to gain the vantage point overlooking Mobile Bay. Eager to leave the dungeon behind, I climbed the steps to join him.

From atop the fort it is easy to see why this site, centuries before, was chosen to safeguard the area. Had enemy ships been approaching, we would have known instantly—there are no hiding places at sea. Cannons still stand atop the fortress ready to defend their ward.

For an hour or more we roamed the fort, peeking into recesses and gazing outward at the sea, trying to envision the time when one of the Civil War's most important battles was fought here in the late summer of 1864. It was then that Confederate and Union naval forces dueled for control of the harbor entrance.

During the famous Battle of Mobile Bay, the Confederates strung underwater mines across the channel to deter the Union fleet. The Confederate defense failed, however, when the unruffled Admiral David Farragut bellowed his command, "Damn the torpedoes, full speed ahead."

A victim of the fiery battle, the Union's *Tecumseh* sank. It remains submerged, layered with silt some 200 yards from shore on the fort's west side. A buoy marks its resting place.

Although Fort Morgan's usefulness declined after the Civil War, the fortification was revitalized and updated as a military base during the Spanish-American War and both World Wars. In 1977 the site was turned over to the state. Today the Alabama Historical Commission oversees the National Military Park.

Although we began first by exploring the fort, it probably is best to begin at the museum, which details the site's history and significance. Exhibits cover military history from the fort's early years through World War II.

After seeing Fort Morgan, we boarded the **Mobile Bay Ferry** for a thirty-minute coastal glimpse of the gulf. A one-way trip saves some 80 miles of highway driving if you are heading from Gulf Shores to Dauphin Island.

As the salt spray bathed my face, the 8-mile ride carried us to **Fort Gaines**, another coastal defense that played an important role in the Battle of Mobile Bay. This star-shaped brick fortress has stood guard at the western approach to Mobile Bay since 1861. Here, several dozen Confederate soldiers were killed or wounded during the 114-hour barrage by Admiral Farragut's forces. Following the Battle of Mobile Bay, Fort Gaines—like Fort Morgan—fell to the Union. You can roam the grounds and explore vaulted tunnels and bastions where Civil War cannons still stand.

Several of the nations that claimed the region in the past built defenses here, beginning with a small wooden fort built by the French in 1717. Later the Spanish and then the English built fortifications on the sight.

The Mobile Bay Ferry (334/540-7787) departs every ninety minutes. As schedules vary by season and prices are subject to change, be sure to call ahead for specific times and costs.

Another of Alabama's famous forts is **Fort Conde** in nearby Mobile. Rebuilt portions of the French fort include a museum and visitors center. Much of the history of Mobile and its Mardi Gras is detailed here.

At Fort Conde, which was occupied by the French from 1717 to 1763, with its low-slung doors and thick walls, you will find facsimiles of eighteenth-century French cannons and muskets, used in demonstrations by guides dressed as French soldiers of that era. Open year-round, the fort displays artifacts excavated from the grounds.

To see yet another of the state's forts, visit **Fort Gilmer** in Russell County. Once used to protect the state's eastern border, the fort remains much the way it was when used by Confederate troops.

Each August reenactments are staged on Mobile Bay. In October reenactors assemble again at Fort Morgan and Fort Gaines to re-create the historic conflict fought there.

For more about Fort Morgan and reenactments call 334/540-7125.

For more about Gulf Shores call 800/745-SAND (7263) or 334/968-7511.

11 ALABAMA GOLF
SWINGING IN THE HEART OF DIXIE

The father of Alabama's public golf courses said it best: "When you start with great land, you end up with great golf courses." Robert Trent Jones Sr., the papa of golf courses, should know. He masterminded more than one-third of the courses chosen by *Golf Digest* as the nation's "100 Greatest Golf Courses."

With his years of experience and success, Jones was a logical choice to become patriarch of a trail of public courses that began opening in Alabama in the early 1900s. By the time the dean of American golf-course architects finished with his handiwork, the state had added 18 courses and 324 holes in 7 separate locations.

Each course in the **Robert Trent Jones Golf Trail** has its own personality, along with a clubhouse that includes meeting or conference rooms, indoor grills, outdoor patios, a dining room, bars, a pro shop, and locker rooms.

Not long after the courses began opening, the *Miami Herald* wrote, "Practically overnight, the Robert Trent Jones Golf Trail has given Alabama one of the finest—and perhaps the finest—collections of golfing facilities anywhere in the South."

Photograph courtesy Robert Trent Jones Golf Trail

Magnolia Grove in Mobile is a southern link in the state's Robert Trent Jones Golf Trail.

Photograph courtesy Robert Trent Jones Golf Trail

Calhoun County's Silver Lakes golf course is part of the Robert Trent Jones Golf Trail.

Any of the courses along the trail can be set up around 7,200 yards to host a major tournament. At the same time the courses average 5,000 yards from the front tees, with as many as 7 tee boxes in between. That allows you to pick the tee best matching your skills.

Each complex includes a Short Course, either with 9 or 18 holes in a par-3 layout. The par-3 holes average 190 yards from the back tees and 90 yards from the front tees, with water hazards, sand bunkers, and tiered greens. The range of diversity appeals both to beginners and to seasoned players.

The trail includes four 54-hole complexes in Birmingham, Mobile, Huntsville, and Auburn/Opelika. In addition there are three 36-hole facilities in Dothan, Greenville, and Calhoun County.

Beginning in the mountains of North Alabama and winding to the Gulf Coast, the courses make up the largest golf-course construction project ever attempted in the world. Daily-fee golfers as well as private-club members have discovered in the heart of Dixie some of the world's greatest golf facilities with affordable prices.

At **Hampton Cove** in Huntsville, players see the mountains from all 54 holes. The Highlands Course has a traditional Scottish style; the River Course runs along the Flint River and includes 26 man-made lakes.

Calhoun County, in northeast Alabama between Gadsden and Anniston, is home to the **Silver Lakes** course. These 36 holes next to the Talladega

National Forest feature a waterfall, large hardwood and pine trees, and many hilltop vistas.

Oxmoor Valley in Birmingham is sculpted from the peaks and valleys of the Appalachian Mountains. These 54 holes offer scenic forests, creeks, and challenging changes in elevation.

Grand National in the Auburn/Opelika area is built amid the 600-acre Lake Saugahatchee, with 32 of the 54 holes bordering water. The Lakes Course, named the fourth-best public course for 1993 by *Golf Digest*, features the signature 15-hole island green.

South of Montgomery, in Greenville, the **Cambrian Ridge** 36-hole facility has more elevation changes than any other courses along the trail. *Golf Digest* in 1994 named the Sherling/Canyon combination as America's third-best new public course.

Dothan's **Highland Oaks** facility has 36 holes on gently rolling terrain that features creeks, swamps, wetlands, oaks, and towering pines. In 1994 *Golf Digest* named the Highlands/Magnolia combination among the nation's seven best new public courses.

Near the Gulf Coast, Mobile's **Magnolia Grove** sprawls on 1,300 acres, where wetlands, creeks, streams, dense pinewoods, and large bunkers characterize its 54 holes. *Golf Digest* has named this course one of the nation's Best Values in the public category.

In late 1998, a new course opened at Prattville, just north of Montgomery. Two more 18-hole courses are planned for that site in 1999, and there is room for a fourth.

All of the courses are within fifteen minutes of an interstate. Although the courses do not have overnight facilities, many local hotels offer individual and group rates. Individuals and groups with fewer than seventeen persons may make tee-time reservations up to forty-five days in advance; larger groups may make reservations up to one year in advance. The trail was developed and is managed by SunBelt Golf Corporation. To purchase passes and schedule tee times call 800/949-4444 or 205/942-0444.

12 MENTONE
DISCOVERING FALL
ON LOOKOUT MOUNTAIN

Mentone, a place the Great God built,
up near the sunlit sky.
Where life is new and friends are true
and days too quickly fly;
Where wearied souls regain their power
and sorrows leave in the night.
Where peace is born with each new morn,
a haven of joy and delight.

—*Sidney Lanier Gibson*

Nowhere in the world are fall colors more beautiful than in North Alabama. And where in the state can you take a more picturesque fall trip than Mentone, the very place that inspired Sidney Lanier Gibson, nephew of poet Sidney Lanier, to pen these words? If you don't yet know what these words mean, you should explore this North Alabama spot where you will find an escape unlike most others.

Photograph by Milton Fullman

In the mountains of North Alabama, Mentone Inn bed-and-breakfast remains a popular retreat.

Photograph by Milton Fullman

Across the street from Mentone Inn, Mentone Springs is a rambling structure with intriguing twists and turns.

In this corner of the state you can hike to a waterfall or overlook a canyon created by a river. A mountaintop town, Mentone's quaint streets are lined with shops and restaurants, many housed in historic buildings. Here you'll find treasures such as dolls made from gourds (called gourdies).

Decades ago visitors were drawn here by the mineral spirits believed to be in the area's warm springwaters. During the tuberculosis scare in the late 1800s, fresh mountain air lured families here. The area developed as a health resort when the John Mason family from Iowa and Dr. Frank Caldwell from Pennsylvania came to be near the healthful springwaters.

While building his home, Dr. Caldwell lived with the Mason family, who helped him name the area. Asked for a suggestion, one of the Mason daughters remembered having read about Queen Victoria's visit to the French town of Mentone, which means "musical mountain spring." The doctor embraced the name as an apt description. The name given to this Lookout Mountain community remains as poignant as ever, as the air here is filled with the sounds of fiddles, church chimes, banjos, and harmonizing voices.

The inn built by Caldwell has changed hands nearly two dozen times, including a period of ownership during the 1980s by an Atlanta Coca-Cola executive and his wife. They restored the multiroom structure, which is now an area landmark.

The nearby **Hitching Post**, once known as the "bloody bucket," dates to the early 1900s. Once a hub for gambling, liquor, and other vices disapproved by local authorities, the building today houses antiques shops and craft stores.

It has been said that Mentone's restaurants belie the area's population. Here you will find everything from pintos and cornbread served in a log cabin to filet mignon available in an elegantly restored farmhouse. "Potluck" is even possible at one of the several charming area inns.

An overnight stay gives you more possibilities since Mentone offers several bed-and-breakfasts. **Blossom Hill B&B** has a separate guest house on Little River Canyon below DeSoto Falls. Adjacent to the **Mentone Wedding Chapel, Mountain Laurel Inn** remains a cherished site for many honeymooners. Other bed-and-breakfast

Photograph by Milton Fullman

Built of fieldstone, Raven Haven in Mentone has five guest rooms, including one dubbed Casablanca.

choices include **Raven Haven,** where one room is called Casablanca because "You must remember this—a room is not just a room," and **Mentone Inn,** which dates to the late 1920s. Here you'll enjoy a main lodge with a wraparound porch, hot tub, and flagstone walks through the flower gardens. The inn has eleven rooms with private baths, plus a separate cottage with three bedrooms.

Mentone, 7 miles from **DeSoto State Park** and only miles from the Georgia state line, is known for its manmade snow. When temperatures cooperate, believe it or not, skiing is possible even here in the Heart of Dixie. April through December, **Cloudmont Ski and Golf Resort** offers golf that is both affordable and spectacular, with the first tee perched atop a 30-foot rock. And when temperatures dip to 28 degrees, snow poofs from machines to cover twin slopes that have a vertical drop of 150 feet. This winter wonderland offers people a place to practice skiing—not a skill most Alabamians grow up learning.

Another of the area's unexpected finds is the **Shady Grove Dude and Guest Ranch.** The state's only dude ranch, Shady Grove was developed as an adjunct to Cloudmont. Here you can hike more than 100 miles of trails and enjoy 2,000 miles of river and wilderness adventure. See page 4 for details.

For more information about Mentone contact the DeKalb County Tourist Association, P.O. Box 681165, Fort Payne, AL 35968-1165; 256/845-3957.

13 MOUNDVILLE
A MOUND OF HISTORY

In the hustle of life today it becomes difficult to envision Indians once roaming and hunting on Alabama land. Anyone who has grown up here probably remembers taking a school field trip to **Moundville Archaeological Park**, site of the once large and powerful southeastern Moundville Indian community. Few places in the state showcase the area's early Indian life like this park, about 12 miles south of Tuscaloosa. Here you can see how these Native Americans held elaborate ceremonies, grew their own foods, and used waterways both for transportation and survival.

The Moundville Indians hauled dirt to build mounds on a bluff overlooking the Black Warrior River. They farmed corn, beans, and squash, and developed a community that grew to include some 3,000 residents. Their everyday life is displayed in a reconstructed village, always a favorite with children.

Although the reason for the mounds remains a mystery, some researchers speculate that they were built as protection from the forces of nature. Others believe they were pedestals for public and ceremonial buildings and residences of honored tribal members. It probably took several communities of people to build the twenty mounds and the wooden palisade used for defense.

Photograph courtesy of Moundville Archaeological Park

An aerial view shows several of the mounds at Moundville Archaeological Park, not far from Tuscaloosa.

The largest mound, which stands some 60 feet high, was the site of a sacred temple, the center of the tribe's religious life. Every July or August people from surrounding villages gathered in the mound community for a festival of the fire/sun god. These festivals were a time of celebration, highlighted by ceremonial dances honoring the gods.

From about A.D. 1000 to A.D. 1500 Moundville was a thriving village. It appears to have been the capital of a group of villages that extended from the area of Tuscaloosa to Demopolis.

Excavated bones indicate that the dead were buried beneath the floors of family dwellings, and some remains have been found in common graves. An old woman and a child share a single grave, while three men and a woman share another plot. Although once available for visitors to view, the remains are no longer made public. Like many other Native Americans, Moundville residents were buried with their most valued possessions, such as swords and pottery.

The museum and park, now owned by the University of Alabama, cover 317 acres and include picnic areas. Be sure to save time to explore the walking trails, where wildflowers and even some smaller mounds are tucked into the woods. You may also want to fish in the ponds in the public areas.

One visitor said: "My favorite time at Moundville is early in the morning when the mists begin to rise off the river. In my mind's eye, I can see the village awaken . . . the women tending the fires, the men repairing their tools, the children and old people starting their daily chores. It's like hearing voices in the wind."

The park is open every day, and the museum is open daily except on major winter holidays. Admission is charged. Nearby you will find camping facilities with water, electrical hookups, tent pads, and grills, as well as picnic tables. For more information call Moundville Archaeological Park at 205/371-2572.

14 ALABAMA DOG AND HORSE TRACKS

THE TROMPING OF FEET

The dogs yelp, scratch the ground, and wait. Then it comes. "Heeeere cooooomes the rabbit," the speaker drawls, as though the greyhounds need to be told.

The dogs know all too well. All they want is the chance to spring from the starting block, to chase that ever-elusive, rabbit-look-alike, which always manages to stay several yards out front.

Betting on dogs and thoroughbreds has become a year-round attraction in Alabama. Although there are opponents to pari-mutuel betting, the sport has found a niche here.

Just west of Mobile, at Exit 13 off I-10, you'll find **Mobile Greyhound Park,** the state's oldest greyhound track, which opened in 1973. During its first twenty years the track generated $100 million for public agencies and proved there was a demand in Alabama for pari-mutuel racing facilities.

Greyhounds race at VictoryLand, between Montgomery and Tuskegee.

Photograph courtesy of Alabama Bureau of Tourism and Travel

When the state gave the nod to its second greyhound track in 1975, skeptics scratched their heads and wondered how a track could survive in Eutaw, a rural west–central Alabama community in one of the state's poorest areas. Since then Eutaw's **Greenetrack** has pumped millions of dollars into a county that needed and has welcomed the income. Today the track offers simulcasts of greyhound races.

Macon County's Greyhound Park, **VictoryLand,** is just beyond Exit 22 off I-85, between Montgomery and Tuskegee. One of the country's most successful grey-hound tracks, it offers year-round entertainment including pari-mutuel betting, out-standing food and beverage service, and thirteen races every performance. The track is one of the state's top traffic-generating, man-made attractions. The focal point of the $20 million facility is VictoryLand's oval track, which helps generate annually several million dollars in taxes.

The Birmingham Race Course offers year-round live greyhound races plus simulcasts of greyhound and thoroughbred races.

This much is for certain, the rabbit always wins. The challenge is knowing which dog will cross the finish line first. And that is anyone's guess!

For more information contact the Alabama Bureau of Tourism and Travel, 800/ALABAMA (252-2262).

1 ANNISTON

M U M M I E S   A N D   M U S E U M S

Never mind that rain pelted the winter day. Never mind that clouds hung overhead. The giant dinosaur, with its huge mouth and teeth to match, seemed to smile down on my husband, our daughter Cameron, and me.

Despite the darkness that hovered over us as we dashed from the car, our moods were transformed when we entered the **Anniston Museum of Natural History,** one of the Southeast's finest collections of natural history specimens. Once inside, we picked our way through a cave to the sounds of dripping water. Heading deeper into the bowels of the "earth," we glanced furtively at sleeping bats above our heads. We shivered and continued on. Caves like this one are all over Alabama, formed throughout millions of years of geological history.

Time moves more quickly in a museum, however. It took fifty people five years to mold this cave, which was constructed using a mile of steel, tons of sand, pounds of plaster and papier-maché, and 1,500 plastic drinking straws. Hardly a task you'd try at home.

The Dynamic Earth Hall is one of several re-creations found in the museum. East African Savannah re-creates that part of the world, with displays of both plant and animal life. Attack and Defense shows how various species protect themselves. The Designs for Living Hall contains an ornithology exhibit that provides a rare opportunity to view species that are now extinct, such as the passenger pigeon, Carolina parakeet, and ivory-billed woodpecker. These birds became part of a naturalist's collection in the 1800s when their species were abundant.

A pair of Egyptian mummies was Cameron's favorite part of the museum. Intrigued, we lingered there longest, reading about these individuals whose wrappings indicate that they were neither wealthy nor poor. The decorations and hieroglyphics indicate that the mummies were embalmed in the third century B.C.

Mummies and dinosaurs wait to be discovered inside the Anniston Museum of Natural History.

Included in the display are X-rays showing that one of the mummies, with a crushed pelvis, lower spine, and ankles, likely died from a fall. This especially intrigued Cameron, I think, because it made these ancient people seem so fragile and vulnerable, almost like us.

She also enjoyed the African continent exhibit. Here more than a hundred African creatures, including an elephant, a black rhinoceros, giraffes, and a zebra, "roam" in dramatic natural settings.

Another permanent exhibit is the Wildlife Garden, planted and designed to attract native wildlife. The paved garden pathways include places where you can rest and absorb the surroundings. Sitting on almost 200 wooded acres, the museum has picnic areas and a mountaintop nature trail that is rife with native Alabama plants and wildlife.

The Museum of Natural History is open daily except Mondays. For more information about the Anniston Museum of Natural History call 256/237-6766.

Although the museum is a highlight of a trip to Anniston, this city offers much more to see.

Don't miss the **Church of St. Michael and All Angels,** built in 1888 entirely of Alabama marble. The ceiling in the central part of the church resembles the ribs of

120

a ship, symbolic of the role of the church in man's spiritual journey. Angel heads carved on the ends of wooden brackets look toward the altar. The Church of St. Michael and All Angels is open for tours except during services.

A recent addition to Anniston, often called "the military showcase of the South," is **Berman Museum.** The museum houses Colonel Farley Berman's lifelong collection of arms, armaments, artwork, and antiquities spanning more than 3,000 years. Included in this tribute to art, history, and weapons are 1,200 bronzes, many by Frederic Remington, 200 paintings, a library of 1,000 volumes, cloisonné artifacts, and 2,000 ancient and modern weapons. Here you can view flutes that fire on a single note, the gun of Charles V of the Holy Roman Empire, Napoleon's good-luck charm, and a bronze ram's helmet worn by a Greek warrior in 300 B.C.

While you're in Anniston you can also visit the **Military Police Corps Regimental Museum,** as well as **Neely Henry Lake,** where you can fish or boat and **Tyler Hill Square Historic District,** a small, square park surrounded by Victorian homes built in the late 1800s.

If you want a quaint place to stay in Anniston, you will enjoy **The Victoria,** where some of the rooms are set in an 1888 historic house. The estate sprawls over almost an entire square block along Anniston's major thoroughfare, Quintard Avenue. For more information about The Victoria call 256/236-0503.

For more about Anniston contact the Calhoun County Convention and Visitors Bureau, P.O. Box 1087, Anniston, AL 36202; 256/237-3536.

2 BLACK HISTORY
IN SEARCH OF ROOTS

Our daughters Christine and Cameron were fortunate to have been born a decade after the civil rights struggles that drew national attention to Birmingham. Living amid racial tolerance and integration, they have grown up with little understanding of those decades. Although we've often talked about the civil rights movement of the 1960s, nothing from that era has hit home as directly as Cameron's visit to the **Birmingham Civil Rights Institute.**

One sunny afternoon we headed to downtown Birmingham to visit the museum, which has become a focal point for the city's role in the civil rights movement. Driving to town Cameron laughed and giggled, as teenagers will. Her mood grew somber, however, as we moved from one interactive exhibit to the other in the museum. It is not easy to learn of man's inhumanity to man. Cameron was transfixed, and I think I observed her response as much as I studied the exhibits themselves.

You will begin your journey on the road to equality at the Institute by watching a film about Birmingham's early years. At the end of the viewing, the screen lifts to reveal drinking fountains labeled "colored" and "white," and you enter the era of segregation. Lifelike figures and detailed exhibits recall the city's mining industry, a streetcar, a shotgun house, a movie theater, and other glimpses of everyday life in a segregated city.

You will experience four dramatic, pivotal moments of the civil rights movement before you join a procession of figures celebrating overdue victories. Your journey will end in a gallery that depicts current human-rights issues. At the exhibit's end you look through large windows at **Sixteenth Street Baptist Church,** where a bomb killed four children on a Sunday morning in 1963, a tragedy that focused the city's, our nation's, and the world's attention on the issues of racial injustice.

Outside the front door of the Civil Rights Institute and across from Sixteenth Street Baptist Church, **Kelly Ingram Park** displays a statue of Martin Luther King Jr., who once marched on these Birmingham streets. Through the years this park has served as a point of origin for marches, rallies, and prayer services.

A stretch of Fourth Avenue North in downtown Birmingham preserves the final remnant of what once was the heart of black social and cultural life. The **Jazz Hall of Fame,** housed in the historic **Carver Theater,** displays exhibits on Nat "King" Cole, Duke Ellington, Erskine Hawkins, and other jazz greats. Visitors travel from the beginnings of boogie-woogie, with Clarence "Pinetop" Smith, to the jazz space journeys of Sun Ra and His Intergalactic Space Arkestra.

You can explore more of the state's black history in Tuscaloosa at the **Murphy African American Museum,** former home of Will Murphy. Born during the era of slavery, Murphy became a successful and wealthy man. His portrait hangs in this two-story bungalow, built in the late 1920s with bricks and beams from the old Alabama State Capitol Building. The museum is eclectic, showcasing an array of threads from the tapestry of Tuscaloosa's black history.

A statue of Dr. Martin Luther King, Jr., stands in Birmingham's Kelly Ingram Park, across from the Civil Rights Institute.

Also be sure to visit the **W. C. Handy Home and Museum** in Florence. Handy, often called the father of the blues, was born in 1873 in this log cabin on West College Street. A museum filled with Handy memorabilia includes his trumpet and the piano he used to compose "St. Louis Blues."

In Limestone County you can visit a **Union fort** once manned by two companies of African-American soldiers. The fort and the railroad trestle were burned by General Nathan Bedford Forrest, who wanted to interfere with the flow of Union supply lines. By assigning African Americans to the fort, the Union Army hoped to free its Caucasian troops for frontline duty.

The Decatur Courthouse in Morgan County is where the "Scottsboro Boys" were retried in 1933. The case led to a landmark Supreme Court ruling that gave a defendant the right to a jury of his peers. This ruling meant that African Americans could serve on a jury.

It doesn't take long to realize that African-American history reveals itself in all forms in Alabama—from monuments to homes, churches to courthouses. Stand silently and you can almost hear the shouts of civil rights marchers, the tunes of jazz singers, and the ringing of church bells.

For more information call the Alabama Bureau of Tourism and Travel, 800/ALABAMA (252-2262). For details about the Birmingham Civil Rights Institute call 205/328-9696. For details about Birmingham call the city's Convention and Visitors Bureau, 800/458-8085 or 205/458-8000.

3   EAGLE AWARENESS AT LAKE GUNTERSVILLE STATE PARK

IF YOU WOULD SOAR WITH THE EAGLES

W hen I was growing up, I often heard my father say, "If you would soar with the eagles in the morning, never hoot with the owls at night." His wisdom grew vivid one winter evening after I had spent a morning at **Lake Guntersville State Park** observing the eagles soaring.

During my eagle-watching trek I learned that these birds, like people heading off to work, leave their nests at the break of dawn. That should give you some indication of the early hour. This explains why owls and eagles have very different timetables.

On the first night of my quest for eagles, I enjoyed a delicious dinner at the state park lodge—an unexpected treat as I had not perceived this place to be a gourmet restaurant. Following dinner, our eagle-watching group gathered in one of the lodge conference rooms to view slides and listen to the director of the **Eagle Awareness program,** naturalist Linda Reynolds, talk about eagles and the program that began in the late 1980s.

In North Alabama, visitors learn about eagles at Lake Guntersville State Park.

125

Following a workday with unending deadlines, I wasn't certain I was hyped for bird talk. But it didn't take long to get into bird-watching. I think what converted me was the excitement shared by other participants, many of whom had already spotted eagles either earlier that day or on previous **Eagle Awareness Weekends.** I eavesdropped as they shared their stories, including one person's admission that he had watched with joy until he realized he had spotted not majestic eagles but ordinary crows.

Much like Northerners who seek winter refuge in the South, eagles migrate to Alabama to wait out the cold. Several of the eagles who winter at Lake Guntersville return year after year to this area, where the days usually are moderate and sunshine is a possibility most anytime.

A native of this region told me that in the 1920s when the eagles would fly overhead on their route south, parents, not certain of the birds' intentions, were quick to grab up their babies and rush them indoors to safety. "We just didn't know what those big birds had in mind," he remembered. In reality all they had on their minds was to find warmth.

"Look for the eagles to fly in horizontal lines close to the water," advised Linda as she prepared us for our outing slated for the following morning.

As we sipped hot cider we learned that decades of wanton killing, encroachment of development, electric power lines, egg collectors, and cars had severely diminished the number of bald eagles, making them almost extinct by 1960. Pesticides and DDT threatened to finish off the majestic birds.

Alabama was not the only state losing eagles. By 1970 twenty-five other states had reported an absence of breeding pairs, and still more had noted a decline. Something had to be done.

Concerned officials resurrected and applied an old international treaty to protect the bald eagles, and in the early 1970s a new Endangered Species Act imposed stiff penalties for disturbing the birds, their nests, or their young.

To help resolve the problem in Alabama, a band of people released almost a hundred eagles. The theory was that the eagles would return each winter to the same place where they had been released. This belief has panned out.

In recent years dozens of eagles have been spotted near Lake Guntersville State Park, a site that has camping, cabins, chalets, tennis, and an 18-hole golf course. The lodge, set on a bluff overlooking a picture-perfect lake, has guest- and meeting rooms, a restaurant, and a coffee shop.

Eagles build huge nests, some as large as a Volkswagen Beetle. Although big sticks are a mainstay, some nests have been discovered with all kinds of materials, from Clorox bottles to "pink panties with lace."

The best time to see an eagle is on cold, overcast days without wind. "But it's not necessarily the best time for people," smiled Linda, who initiated Lake Guntersville's Eagle Awareness program, now so popular that winter weekends at the lodge sell out. "You have to work hard to find the eagles," she challenged during her first-night presentation. However, she admitted, a dose of luck is another prerequisite for spotting one of the mighty birds.

It was pitch dark when the unwelcome alarm clock woke me on a clear but cold morning at the lodge. With sleepy eyes my friend and I groped our way to the lodge's rustic lobby, where others in the group had already gathered for morning coffee. There we traded caffeine for the sleep we were missing.

Before our departure Linda reminded us of the procedures spelled out the night before. We would get in our cars and follow her lead off the tip of Little Mountain. When we arrived at the viewing site, we were to turn off our headlights and slip from our vehicles without talking or slamming doors. We were to take our places alongside the highway at a point that overlooks the winding Tennessee River, a tiny island, and a tree-studded mountain.

There we were to wait.

At our viewing spot, we stood in the dark and silence that was shattered only by an occasional passing vehicle. Shivering in the cold, I drew my coat tightly around me. I stared into the dark, wondering if an eagle could be worth this much effort.

Fingers of light began to sprawl across the dark sky. For one of the many days of my forty-something years that I have been up at the break of dawn, this time I had broken dawn.

As light began to flood the hillside, we saw nothing. We heard an occasional cawing in the distance. I didn't know if it was an eagle, but I looked more intently now that I had the promise that one might fly past.

My friend and I whispered, drawing haughty looks from some of the others in our group who wondered how we could desecrate the silence. We wondered why we were here, standing in the cold dark of the morning.

Then, as suddenly as a meteor races to earth, they were before us—two eagles as majestic and regal as their image could have promised. Just as Linda had predicted, the eagles had left their nests to venture out for food.

We raised binoculars and whispered to each other ever so quietly, as though to say more would frighten the birds or break some kind of spell. In unison our heads moved from left to right, up a bit, down a bit. Binoculars and heads followed the flight pattern, working to absorb every fleeting second.

That's when I knew why I had forgone sleep and defied common sense to come here. I had seen an eagle in his environment, on his timetable. It was a moment I shall never forget. For a city girl, I felt almost at one with nature.

My friend and I whispered again. This time the cold did not seem so cold, and the hour did not seem so early. Like explorers of long ago, we had found what we had been looking for.

Although some years eagles remain in North Alabama until February or early March, Lake Guntersville's Eagle Awareness program is held in January, on weekends and once midweek. Weekend packages include two nights at the lodge, an apple-cider social and eagle orientation, early-bird coffee, a Saturday-night banquet, and guided observation tours for chances to spot not just eagles but other birds. The midweek program includes a Tuesday night apple-cider social, the bird program, coffee, and observation trips. If you prefer not to stay overnight you can, at no charge, look for eagles on your own or join one of the guided groups.

Once the days begin to warm and the eagles head north again, you can visit the park for fishing, boating, camping, golf, hiking, tennis, and just about anything else you can imagine doing in a nature wonderland. Many people come here for meetings and family reunions.

For details about Lake Guntersville State Park Lodge call 800/LGVILLE (548-4553) or 256/571-5440; or write 1155 Lodge Drive, Guntersville, AL 35976.

4 HISTORIC SITES
DIGGING FOR ALABAMA'S ROOTS

Sometimes the bits and pieces that are Alabama seem like the ragged parts of a tattered weaving. But if you put the varied sections together and gaze upon the total picture, you'll discover a gorgeous tapestry. If you want to know what is woven together to make the fabric that is Alabama, you have only to look into the state's historic sites.

NORTH ALABAMA

You can begin to explore Alabama's early years at **Noccalula Falls Park** near Gadsden. Linked to Native American folklore and the state's earliest settlers, the site is named for a Native American maiden who plunged to her death when she was not allowed to marry the warrior she loved. The state park includes campgrounds, botanical gardens, and a Pioneer Village. The park's pioneer homestead, with its hand-hewn log buildings, shows what life was like for the God-fearing people who lived in the Appalachian foothills.

Further evidence of the Indians who once lived in Alabama has been found at **Russell Cave National Monument**, where excavations have unearthed remains of campfires made by Native Americans who lived here thousands of years ago.

CENTRAL ALABAMA

Plan time to visit Alabama's first capital at **Cahawba**, later renamed Cahaba. Near Selma, Cahaba grew rapidly while it was the center of the state's politics, but floods and disease eventually devastated the once-thriving community.

The old **Brierfield Iron Works**, preserved in **Tannehill State Park** not far from Birmingham, roared during the Civil War in an attempt to furnish equipment to Confederate troops.

Photograph by Milton Fullman

A Confederate cemetery is a reminder of Alabama's earlier years.

The furnaces burned until Christmas Eve 1894 when the owners went bankrupt. Today the park has a country store, a picnic area, camping facilities, and hiking trails.

Not long after **Sloss Furnaces** were built in 1882, iron began to flow from these open-hearth furnaces that sit just east of downtown Birmingham. Today a museum and community center, Sloss Furnaces National Historic Landmark remind everyone of the industry that gave Birmingham its start.

Confederate Memorial Park in Chilton County vividly recalls events of the Civil War. The Confederate museum houses records, documents, and photographs associated with the Confederate Soldiers' Home that once stood on the site.

In Tuscaloosa, the site of the state's second permanent capital, you will find **Gorgas House**, a two-story brick, Federal-style cottage that survived the Civil War to become one of the country's oldest college structures.

Photograph by Milton Fullman

Built in the mid-1800s, Sturdivant Hall in Selma is one of Alabama's grand mansions.

The intrigue of the plantation region reaches beyond Tuscaloosa's boundaries. In fact some of the region's grandest and most historic structures are found in the Black Belt, named for its dark and fertile soil. Early settlers who farmed the land here became wealthy planters and built mansions such as **Gaineswood**, as well as **Bluff Hall** in Demopolis, **Magnolia Grove** in Greensboro, **Sturdivant Hall** in Selma, **Holman Mansion** in Ozark, and those in the **Lowndesboro Historic District**. Other old and stately homes bordering the plantation region include **Buena Vista Mansion** in Prattville, the state's only remaining **octagon house** in Clayton, and Eufaula's **Shorter Mansion**.

SOUTH ALABAMA

At Prichard in South Alabama you can visit **AfricaTown U.S.A. State Park,** the first state park to acknowledge our nation's African-American history. The park pays tribute to passengers of the *Clotilde*, the last known vessel to carry Africans destined for slavery in this country.

Just as it is not possible to identify every thread woven into a tapestry, it would be difficult to visit all the historic sites that have made Alabama what it is today. Even so, glimpses from the sites described above will show you how the tapestry was woven from this land dotted with winding rivers, blooming azaleas, and roots running deep into the soil.

For information on sites in North Alabama call the Alabama Mountain Lakes Association at 800/648-5381. For details on Noccalula Falls and the surrounding area call the Gadsden–Etowah Tourism Board at 256/549-0351. For details on Montgomery sites call the city's convention and visitor development office at 334/240-9453. For information on other sites contact the Alabama Bureau of Tourism and Travel at 800/ALABAMA (252-2262).

5 MARION
ARCHITECTURAL MARVELS

Scarlett and Rhett surely would have felt at home among the columned homes of Marion. Tours here, most of which must be prearranged, take you through a host of majestic old houses.

Be sure to visit the **Lovelace-Lewis House**, a Greek Revival structure that retains most of its original features plus original Victorian gardens; the **Lowery-Henry House**; the **Myatt-Duck House**, a Victorian home; and **Reverie**, an 1858 home with ornate plasterwork and circular columns made of pie-shaped brick.

Other must-see sites in Marion include:

The **Perry County Courthouse** displays the marriage license of Sam Houston, a hero of the war against Mexico.

The **Congregationalist Church**, was built in 1870 as part of the all-black Lincoln School that educated freed slaves.

The **Old City Hall**, now moved to the Marion campus, houses the **Alabama Military Hall of Honor.**

Confederate Rest is a site where both Union and Confederate soldiers are buried, many of whom were wounded during the Battle of Selma in 1865. The bodies were disinterred in 1872 and moved from the hospital grounds to a section of the cemetery behind St. Wilfrid's church.

Marion Military Institute dates to 1846. Spend a few quiet minutes in the historic Marion Military Institute Chapel, which served as a hospital during the Civil War.

Marion Female Seminary, dating to 1836, is one of only a dozen antebellum school buildings remaining in Alabama. An instructor at the seminary in 1860 designed the original Confederate flag and uniform displayed in this building.

The **Alabama Women's Hall of Fame** was established at **Judson College** in 1970 to recognize women who played a key role in Alabama history. To be selected for membership a woman must have made a significant contribution on a state, national, or international scale within her field.

The **Carlisle-Hall-Martin Mansion**, designed by a New York architect, has three stories and a tower that combine Gothic, Romanesque, Moorish, and Japanese architectural styles. This house has attracted curious students from the Smithsonian Institution.

The Alabama Women's Hall of Fame is housed on the Judson College campus.

Harry's monument in **Marion Cemetery** honors a servant who died while rousing Marion students during a fire.

You will also find here the home of secession governor **Andrew Barry Moore** and headquarters of **General Nathan Bedford Forrest.**

Antiques and Co., a nationally known antiques shop, is housed in a building that dates to 1848.

The Gateway Inn, with good food at good prices, shows a bit of county history in the architectural details used to renovate the facility.

For more information about Marion call the Perry County Chamber of Commerce at 334/683-9622 or the Alabama Bureau of Tourism and Travel at 800/ALABAMA (252-2262).

6 MONTGOMERY
THE STAGE FOR CIVIL WAR
AND CIVIL RIGHTS

A stage crew would be kept busy changing backdrops and transforming sets in a play about the history of Montgomery, Alabama's state capital. The opening scene might be the one that sealed the city's destiny—the inauguration of Jefferson Davis as president of the Confederacy. Within a few months of the inauguration, the South's capital moved to Richmond—but Montgomery had already secured its place in history.

Act Two could focus on the Davises, set against **the first White House of the Confederacy.** It was there that the Davises made their home and hosted lively dinners before moving to Richmond in 1861. The house, later moved to its present location within the shadow of the capitol building, is filled today with period furnishings and many Davis family belongings.

A permanent backdrop in this city is the domed **capitol building.** Renovated in the early 1990s, this stately structure is where former Governor George Wallace made his now-famous "Segregation Today, Segregation Tomorrow, and Segregation Forever" speech that brought national attention to the civil rights struggle.

Scenes from the civil rights movement provide another backdrop for much of what has been staged in Montgomery. That era is remembered with the **Civil Rights Memorial,** which lists the names of those who died during the movement. You can trail your fingertips through the water that spills across the names.

Photograph by Milton Fullman

The capitol building centers downtown Montgomery.

Be sure to visit **Dexter Avenue–King Memorial Baptist Church,** which is within walking distance of the capitol. The state's first NAACP convention was held at this church in 1945, which, during much of the civil rights movement, served as a meeting place and focal point for activists. You will begin your tour downstairs, where a mural details the road to civil rights. You can also watch a video that will prepare you for what you will see upstairs, and you can stand in the pulpit where Dr. Martin Luther King Jr. once stood.

Scenes of the city's early years are preserved at **Old Alabama Town** in downtown Montgomery. This re-creation of houses and landscapes demonstrates how people here lived from 1800 to 1900. Your tour

Photograph by Milton Fullman

The first White House of the Confederacy is where the Confederacy's only president, Jefferson Davis, lived briefly before moving to Richmond.

begins at **Lucas Tavern,** where many a pioneer supped. Then you walk through a pole barn into a log cabin where settlers once lived. From there you enter a one-room schoolhouse and participate in vanishing skills as craftspeople perform their tasks.

Be sure to look for the following Montgomery sites even though they are not related to the Civil War or civil rights.

The F. Scott Fitzgerald Museum on Felder Avenue is the world's only museum dedicated to this writer. The Fitzgeralds rented this house for a short period, and it now contains some of the couple's artifacts, including Zelda Fitzgerald's artworks.

The Museum of Fine Arts, nestled in a lake-studded parkland, houses spacious galleries filled with nineteenth- and twentieth-century paintings, European and American works on paper, as well as drawings, etchings, engravings, and other graphics. You will also see a kids' hands-on gallery and art studio, which some adults find intriguing. Save time for lunch served in the museum's **Terrace Cafe.**

Adjacent to the museum is the **Alabama Shakespeare Festival,** a multimillion-dollar, two-theater complex. You can tour this fully professional facility and see one of the performances that are staged year-round.

If you're a country-music fan, you'll want to visit **Hank Williams' grave** in **Oakwood Cemetery Annex,** off Upper Wetumpka Road in downtown Montgomery.

The stage is set in Montgomery, ready to give you the opportunity to delve into the Civil War and civil rights days that ensured this Southern city its place in history. If you would like to stay in a bed-and-breakfast when you visit Montgomery, try **Red Bluff Cottage** (334/264-0056), which overlooks the Alabama River.

For more about Montgomery call the convention and visitors development office at 334/240-9453 or the Alabama Bureau of Tourism and Travel at 800/ALABAMA (252-2262).

7 MOORESVILLE
NO TRAINS ALLOWED

Opportunity is everything, and today you have to wonder if the early settlers of Mooresville, in North Alabama, knew what they were missing when they decided against allowing the railroad to come through their tree-shaded hamlet.

Settled by cotton planters, Mooresville is the state's second-oldest town (Mobile is the oldest). When Mooresville refused to allow the railroad to come, the town was stunted, never growing beyond its 1-square-mile boundaries. The entire town, which has only a few dozen residents, is listed on the National Register of Historic Places and is a virtual museum of houses dating to the early 1800s.

There are no tourist traps in this village some 85 miles north of Birmingham, midway between Decatur and Huntsville. Yet even though the town is small, it attracts plenty of attention, in part because time seems to have stood still here.

In the spring of 1995, Painted Fences Productions' film crews moved into Mooresville to film the movie *Tom Sawyer.* They used the hamlet for the town scenes of Hannibal, Missouri. The film's other Alabama locations include Wheeler Wildlife Refuge and Cathedral Caverns.

Photograph courtesy of Alabama Mountain Lakes Tourist Association

In Mooresville, horse-and-buggy rides are one way to explore this North Alabama town during its biannual home tours.

"Mooresville is a unique town and deserves to be preserved on film," Ross Fanger, Painted Fences' production manager said not long after the announcement was made that Mooresville had been chosen.

The movie and the town were a perfect match, with the story set in 1845 and the historic **Mooresville post office** having been built in 1843. Before production could begin, sets were built to depict the commercial and residential districts of Hannibal. The production company used many existing buildings in Mooresville and added other facades and porches.

A crew several dozen strong was involved with the making of the film starring Brad Renfroe as Huck Finn and Jonathan Taylor Thomas, of TV's *Home Improvement*, as Tom Sawyer. Although the filmmakers and young stars have moved on, Mooresville remains a city worth the visit.

You can discover this historic town by car or by foot. To understand and interpret what you see along your tour, stop by the Mooresville post office, open Monday through Saturday, 7:30 a.m. to 1:15 p.m., to pick up a booklet detailing the town.

In addition to the houses and buildings on the walking tour, several other points of interest are included in the booklet.

Broad Street leads to the old **Mooresville Cemetery,** where Union and Confederate soldiers are buried.

The spring that gave the town its original water supply can be reached from the south end of **Market Street.**

A tailor shop owned by Joseph Sloss stands on the southwest corner of Piney and Market Streets. Sloss' specialty was the Prince Albert–style coat—a men's double-breasted coat with a full skirt that reached to the knees. Young Andrew Johnson, who later became the nation's seventeenth president, was in Mooresville sometime between 1826 and 1835 to study under Sloss.

Visit the old church where a psychic minister and James Garfield preached, and a tavern and stagecoach inn that once welcomed weary travelers.

If you plan to stay overnight, your best bet is to head to **Madison,** ten minutes away. Try the catfish and hushpuppies at nearby **Greenbrier Barbecue.** Before you head for home you might want to continue on to explore sites in nearby Huntsville and Decatur.

For more information call the Alabama Mountain Lakes Tourist Association, 800/648-5381.

8 ROMANTIC PLACES
LOOKING FOR LOVE
IN ALL THE RIGHT PLACES

When Valentine's Day rolls around, most of us have romance on our minds. Well, most everyone. My husband, Milton, is not the romantic kind. So that leaves the challenge to me to find romantic places and activities. Thank goodness for Alabama, where there are plenty of special places for people in love.

When planning a romantic weekend getaway, don't try to include too much. Once you've chosen your destination, save time just for the two of you. You might want to sleep in a four-poster bed, sip champagne, or walk hand-in-hand. Maybe you and yours prefer a chalet nestled in the woods, a candlelit dinner, and an after-dinner stroll.

No matter how you spend a romantic weekend, remember that love, according to Ralph Waldo Emerson, "is the essence of God, is not for levity, but for the total worth of man."

I offer the following suggestions for those celebrating Cupid's conquests in Alabama.

One of Birmingham's most romantic places is **Vulcan Park**, home of the city's most visible statue, which overlooks the city from atop Red Mountain. Pack

Photograph by Milton Fullman

Photograph by Milton Fullman

DeSoto Falls, above, and Little River Canyon, right, are favorite spots for lovers.

a picnic and arrive at twilight. Ride the elevator—or take the stairs if you're feeling energetic—and get a sky view of downtown.

In northeast Alabama, **Little River Canyon** ends in a tumbling plunge over **DeSoto Falls**. Stay the night and prepare your own candlelit dinner in a cabin or chalet at nearby **DeSoto State Park**. As the candles flicker, sip champagne by the fire and the next day head outdoors to enjoy Mother Nature.

Similar accommodations can be found at **Lake Guntersville State Park**. Or choose **Tannehill Ironworks Historical State Park** if you prefer a more rustic cabin and a chance to ride horseback.

The pounding surf along Alabama's Gulf Coast has long lured those seeking romance.

Visit **Palisades Park**, near Oneonta, for a chance to stand atop an 80-foot bluff and view the mountains in the distance.

You can go to Blount County and sneak a kiss at one of the three covered bridges where lovers, even in the bridges' early years, stole a few kisses beneath their shelter.

Although the beaches on Alabama's Gulf Coast are special year-round, the crowds thin and rates for accommodations drop in winter months. February is a good time to visit Gulf Shores and stroll the beach. If chilly waters don't concern you, take off your shoes, roll up your pant legs, and poke your toes into the water.

You may also want to visit the **Alabama Music Hall of Fame** in Tuscumbia, where exhibits spotlight music greats with Alabama ties. You can cut your own track in the sound booth and take home an audio reminder of the time the two of you made sweet music.

Photograph by Milton Fullman

In Florence you can dine atop the **Renaissance Tower.** Request a table for two with a view of the lock and dam.

If you and your honey met at one of the Alabama's colleges, stroll the campus of your alma mater and revisit old hangouts. Nowhere are the campuses more postcard perfect than at the **University of Montevallo, Samford University,** and **Tuskegee College.** For old-time's sake, dine in the school cafeteria, visit the bookstore, or just sit beneath a shade tree and reminisce.

Also visit Demopolis, a Black Belt town with lovely old homes, including **Bluff Hall** and **Gaineswood,** which are open for tours. Spend a night at **Riverview Inn** following dinner at **The Foscue House,** between Selma and Demopolis. This rustic restaurant was created by joining two mercantile stores that have exposed brick and plaster walls. Bypass the wooden chairs and ask for a booth or a table close to the potbellied stove in the center of the dining area. Opt for the house specialty of steak and baked potato.

You will find another romantic spot in Eufaula, one of Alabama's most historic towns. Stay overnight at **Kendall Manor Inn,** a bed-and-breakfast on a hillside, 2 blocks from downtown. A stay includes a welcome drink in the library and afternoon tea. And when you aren't relaxing at Kendall, which dates to the 1860s, explore Eufaula.

For help in planning your romantic getaway, call Alabama State Parks, 800/ALA-PARK (252-7275); Greater Birmingham Convention and Visitors Bureau, 800/458-8085 or 205/458-8000; Demopolis Area Chamber of Commerce, 334/289-0270; Florence, Lauderdale Tourism, 256/740-4141; and Eufaula, Barbour County Tourism Council, 800/524-PLAY (7529) or 334/687-5283.

9 U.S. SPACE AND ROCKET CENTER
FLY ME TO THE MOON

The **U.S. Space and Rocket Center** in Huntsville, Alabama, displays towering earthbound rockets. Although their soaring days are over, these missiles once ripped through the atmosphere in America's pursuit of other realms. One of the state's most popular attractions, the center contains the world's largest collection of missiles, space equipment, and other space-related items.

In the 1950s in Huntsville, Wernher von Braun and other scientists developed the nation's first large, guided missiles. The following decade, von Braun's team designed the rockets that carried U.S. astronauts to the moon. Many of von Braun's papers, photographs, and memorabilia are among the space-related treasures on display.

Huntsville's multimillion-dollar U.S. Space and Rocket Center gives you a chance to experience the sights, sounds, and sensations much like those the astronauts encounter. You can pull levers, push buttons, and strap yourselves into seats to emulate the feel of being propelled into space.

You can also pilot a spacecraft to the moon, ignite a rumbling rocket engine, and feel the forces of gravity tugging to hold you earthbound. You also will have the chance to control a gyro chair and slip into a space helmet. Children can tinker with the hands-on exhibits, and adults can touch a capsule that once splashed returning astronauts into the ocean.

The U.S. Space and Rocket Center is open daily 9 a.m. to

Photograph by Milton Fullman

Towering rockets outside the U.S. Space and Rocket Center make the nation's space program come to life.

5 p.m. Admission is charged. Space camps are available for both children and adults. Call 800/63-SPACE (77223).

Although the space center will amuse you for hours, be sure to allow time to see Huntsville's many other attractions.

Fluted stone columns from the 1914 Madison County Courthouse mark the entrance to the **Botanical Gardens,** located near the U.S. Space and Rocket Center. The fragrance and beauty of the rose gardens alone are worth the visit.

Burritt Museum and Park, once home to a prominent physician, stands atop Monte Sano Mountain overlooking Huntsville. Uniquely built, the house has walls filled with 2,200 bales of wheat straw for insulation. Antiques fill the home's large parlor, and other rooms display Native American artifacts and surgical instruments. The pioneer buildings behind the house are used for special events.

Monte Sano State Park, which sprawls over a couple of thousand acres not far from Burritt Museum, offers a Japanese teahouse, picnic spots, cabins, and scenic overlooks.

The Museum of Art in downtown Huntsville houses hundreds of works, including paintings, sculptures, and historical and contemporary prints. Here you will also find a small collection of furniture, paintings, watercolors, crafts, and other media by artists with Alabama connections.

The Episcopal Church of the Nativity, a block from Huntsville's courthouse square, dates to 1859. This was the only church Union troops did not take over during their occupation of the city during the Civil War.

You can see one of the South's most-concentrated neighborhoods of antebellum homes in **Twickenham Historic District.** Even though only one house is open to the public, you will find the district intriguing on either a driving or walking tour.

10 ALABAMA'S TENNESSEE VALLEY
A RIVER RUNS THROUGH IT

Alabama's northeast corner is the place to discover Mother Nature at her best. The area's subterranean caves have long attracted explorers, and the abundance of water gives you plenty of opportunities for playing—whether swimming, boating, canoeing, water-skiing, kayaking, or whitewater rafting. Although they are not major tourist attractions, Albertville, Arab, Boaz, and Lake Guntersville have an appeal all their own.

Lake Guntersville State Park, one of the area's most popular attractions, sprawls beside Alabama's largest lake, a brainchild of the Tennessee Valley Authority. The park includes thousands of acres of sparkling water amid the Appalachian foothills, creating covers, inlets, and miles of beaches. When the days turn sunny, the park becomes a beehive of activity.

With affordable overnight prices, Lake Guntersville State Park offers golf, swimming, beaches, pools, a campground, picnic areas, tennis courts, hiking trails, canoeing, and fishing facilities. The wood-and-rock lodge may not be rustic, but it looks as though it should be. Rooms, chalets, and cabins are roomy, and many offer memorable views of the forests and winding river below.

Boaz, about 25 miles away, features several major retail outlet centers and 150 factory outlet stores. It's a place where you can truly shop until they have to scoop you up.

You may be glad you don't live in **Russell Cave National Monument,** but for some 8,000 years plenty of people called the area home. The monument, made famous after magazine coverage in the early 1950s reported its excavation, details thousands of years of life. The cave itself

Photograph by Milton Fullman

Although Russell Cave National Monument extends for miles, visitors may only glimpse its opening.

Photograph by Milton Fullman

The Old State Bank in Decatur still has its original vault.

extends several miles into the limestone mountain, where tools, bones, and other debris have helped chronicle the past. A fence prevents you from going beyond the cave's mouth, which means there's neither danger nor access to places where the curious might choose to explore. You can view an exhibit, however, and watch a brief program in the cave shelter.

Decatur lies southwest of Huntsville, where the Tennessee River's influence has been potent, lending its power for industrial growth and recreational activities. Be sure to visit the historic district between the river and Lee Street. This Victorian neighborhood, which is canopied with towering oaks and laced with sidewalks, includes the historic **Bank Street** commercial area and the restored **Old State Bank**, once a branch of a statewide system. Look for the original vault on the building's first floor.

East of Decatur you will find **Point Mallard**, a huge recreation park carved into land where Flint Creek flows from the Tennessee River. When the park opened, it sported the nation's first wave pool. The complex includes a diving pool and tower, a squirt factory, a three-flume waterslide, picnic spots, a playground, miniature golf, and a sandy beach. On warm days the park provides a day's worth of fun.

Photograph by Milton Fullman

Young visitors are fascinated by displays at Wheeler Wildlife Refuge.

Sprawling between Huntsville and Decatur, **Wheeler National Wildlife Refuge** provides the winter home for Alabama's largest concentration of ducks and Canada geese. These 34,500 acres are pocked with mudflats, swamps, hardwoods, an observation building and visitors center, foot trails, a waterfowl observation platform, a boardwalk, and grounds for picnicking, boating, hunting, and fishing.

The might and power of rivers are awesome. If you don't believe it, just take a closer look at what the Tennessee River has done for the northern part of Alabama. Good thing the highways and byways through this region form a network for exploration—a canoe trip here would be a bit tiring.

For more information about this area call Alabama Mountain Lakes Association, 800/648-5381; Boaz Chamber of Commerce, 256/593-8154; Chamber of Commerce of the Shoals, 256/764-4661; Cullman County Convention and Tourism Bureau, 256/734-0454; Huntsville/Madison County Convention and Visitors Bureau, 800/SPACE-4-U (772-2348); Lake Guntersville Chamber of Commerce, 256/582-3612; Marshall County Tourism Commission, 256/582-7015; or the Alabama Bureau of Tourism and Travel, 800/ALABAMA (252-2262).

11 UNION SPRINGS
A HANGING PLACE

There is something eerie about walking inside the old jail in Union Springs. The dark brick exterior, turrets, and rustic stone make it seem more like a brooding castle than a place that once housed criminals.

You can almost hear the voices of prisoners held in cubicles that are much too small for man or beast. It is easy to imagine the screaming voices, the discontent, the fracases that took place in the bull pen—an open area that allowed some freedom of movement. It is here that longtime inmates harassed and beat newcomers to extract cigarettes or cash.

Most haunting of all are the gallows and trapdoor that remain on the jail's third floor. Here prisoners met their deaths, after which their bodies were hauled out the narrow front door as other prisoners surely looked on from their cells. Be especially careful when you tour the third floor because the trapdoor remains operational.

The **Bullock County Jail** was built in 1897, in the days when convicted criminals were allowed little more than food and a place to sleep. Several years ago, after having been abandoned in 1979, the jail faced almost certain destruction until a band of people determined that the structure should be preserved and used as a museum.

Known as Pauly Jail, the structure, which housed the insane as well as male and female prisoners, was considered the most modern of its era. On the first level you will see the jailer's living quarters, which

Photograph by Milton Fullman

The old jail in Union Springs can be a creepy place to visit.

147

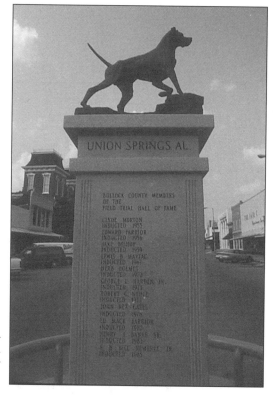

UNION SPRINGS, AL.

BULLOCK COUNTY MEMBERS
OF THE
FIELD TRIAL HALL OF FAME

CLYDE MORTON
INDUCTED 1955
EDWARD FARRIOR
INDUCTED 1956
JAKE BISHOP
INDUCTED 1959
LEWIS P. MAYTAG
INDUCTED 1965
HERB HOLMES
INDUCTED 1970
GEORGE L. HARRISON JR.
INDUCTED 1973
ROBERT C. WEHLE
INDUCTED 1977
JOHN REX GATES
INDUCTED 1978
ED MACK FARRIOR
INDUCTED 1982
NERO
INDUCTED 1983
A. B. WHILE JR.(WILEY JR.)
INDUCTED 1985

Photograph by Milton Fullman

A field-dog monument stands in downtown Union Springs.

were heated in winter with a coal-burning fireplace and cooled in summer with whatever breeze managed to waft between the bars barricading the windows.

Women were housed on the same floor as the jailer, and the two upper levels housed the men, who lived in cramped quarters that sometimes held four men in a space as small as some of today's closets.

Converted in 1995 into a museum with a growing collection of items relating to the county's history, the twelve-cell jail is also used for social functions and special events, a much different atmosphere from which existed during the decades when renegades were kept behind its locked doors.

The jail sits behind the courthouse adjacent to a park and gazebo. If weather permits you can spread a picnic here before touring this hamlet of turn-of-the-century homes, churches, and other buildings.

Park downtown somewhere in the 100 to 200 blocks of North Prairie Street and walk up and down the street to see some of the county's most historic structures. Be sure to stop and see **Trinity Episcopal Church** with its Gothic arches and stained-glass windows. In **Old City Cemetery** at the rear of the church a monument overlooks graves of both Yankee and Rebel soldiers. Nearby you'll find an old log cabin museum, open only by appointment, that is authentically furnished, and with a rock fireplace and chimney.

Other must-sees include the **1912 Carnegie Library** with its many original furnishings, chandeliers, and mahogany woodwork. Nearby you'll find **First Baptist Church**, which was established in 1849; the 1859 wood frame remains in place beneath the present-day brick facade. Across from the church you'll see the **Josephine Hotel,** dating to 1880 when it was named for the builder's wife.

Bullock County Courthouse stands in front of the jail in the downtown historic district. It dates to 1871 and was patterned after the Old Executive Office Building in Washington, D.C.

Main Drug Store, the first brick building erected on Prairie Street, dates to 1867. It was used as a mercantile store and had a saloon in the basement. Resembling a modern drugstore inside, you'll find here an impressive collection of gift items.

After your downtown walking tour, head to your car for a riding tour of the surrounding residential communities, including the North Prairie residential district, a ridge area that was the site of early settlement.

While some visitors are intrigued by the town's historic feel, others come for the town's field-dog trials, which draw national attention. Some of the trials take place at the 14,000-acre **Sedgefield Plantation,** which is considered to be the world's best bird-dog field trial grounds. Union Springs has erected a monument to the field dog, which stands in the downtown historic district.

Bullock County has several options for hunters, including riding with the hounds at **Fitzpatrick Fox Hunts;** quail hunting from vehicle, horseback, or on foot at **Gunsmoke Kennels;** and white-tailed deer hunting on 10,000 acres at **Master Rack Lodge.**

You could spend the second leg of your weekend in this southeastern segment of the state exploring nearby **Fort Mitchell.** The fort, off Alabama Highway 165 in Russell County, was built by General John Floyd as a staging center for operations against the Creek Indians. Eventually abandoned and then rebuilt in 1825, the site served as an assembly point for Indians being removed to the West. A series of markers interpret the historic site.

Fort Mitchell National Cemetery, adjacent to **Fort Mitchell County Park,** is a 280-acre historic site often called "the Arlington of the South." It provides the final resting place for veterans of the U.S. military forces.

Opened in 1996, the **Chattahoochee Indian Heritage Center** inside Fort Mitchell County Park includes a re-created Indian ball field, a nature trail with native plants used by the Indians, and a sacred fire sculpture. The names of some 3,000 Indians removed from the area in the 1830s are inscribed on arbors flanking the sculpture.

Not far from Union Springs in Clayton you will find two conversation pieces sure to make you a hit at your next social gathering. **The Octagon House** on North

Midway Street is the state's only antebellum example of this unusual architecture. Built with 18-inch stone-and-gravel walls, the house is open by appointment only, but it is worth driving by even if you don't go inside. The other conversation piece sits in the **Clayton Baptist Church Cemetery,** where a whiskey bottle tombstone marks the resting place of W. T. Mullen, who died in 1863. According to legend, Mullen was a heavy drinker. His wife threatened to—and did—erect a vertical whiskey bottle as his tombstone if he drank himself to death.

From jail to grave marker to antebellum homes, this piece of Alabama makes a fun getaway off the beaten path and away from life's maddening pace. Escape highway traffic and bustling crowds. Kick back and enjoy this slow-paced weekend while you explore some of the state's roots. Find a piece of Americana that time has almost forgotten.

Each February 22, Union Springs hosts the nation's largest amateur field-dog trials. The town also hosts an annual pilgrimage and historic-home tours on the first Saturday and Sunday of May. One of the town's most popular annual events is the **Chunnenuggee Fair,** held the first Saturday in May in the business district, where arts and crafts and spring wares from local and regional vendors abound.

When you visit Union Springs and Clayton, your best bet is to stay overnight either in Montgomery, 45 miles away; in Troy, 35 miles south; or in Eufaula, some 30 miles east. (Eufaula has wonderful bed-and-breakfasts, including **Kendall Manor Inn.**)

You will find other adventures at **Bluff Creek Park,** off Alabama Highway 165 south of Phenix City. This federal recreational area along the Chattahoochee River has a boat ramp, tent and trailer camping, a playground, and fishing.

For more information about Union Springs call the Union Springs/Bullock County Tourism Council, 334/738-5411. For more about other areas call the Historic Chattahoochee Commission, 334/687-9755.

12 HOLIDAY CELEBRATIONS
CHRISTMAS IN DIXIE

If Christmas means lights, celebrations, and festivities, then Alabama's rivers and streets are the place to capture the season.

NORTH ALABAMA

Lake Guntersville in northeast Marshall County provides the setting for a **Parade of Lights** boat parade.

Huntsville holds its **Parade of Lights** on the Tennessee River. The parade includes decorated and lighted boats.

Gadsden hosts **Lights on the Coosa**, a riverboat parade. In addition the riverboat **Alabama Princess** offers a 75-minute **Santa Candy Cane Cruise** along the Coosa River.

In **Decatur** you will find a **holiday tour of historic homes** opened for evening tours on select nights during December.

Joe Wheeler State Park Resort hosts the **Rogersville Parade of Lights**.

Oneonta's Second Avenue East is the stage for a countywide Christmas parade.

Moulton holds a downtown **Christmas Parade** with floats, bands, clowns, and Santa.

Arab and **Athens** also hold Christmas parades.

CENTRAL ALABAMA

Demopolis annually hosts a **Christmas on the River Parade** with decorated boats floating down the Tombigbee River. As fireworks explode overhead, boats skim across the river while tiny lights create animated nighttime floats that cast dazzling reflections on dark waters. The parade climaxes a week of festivities that include a crafts fair, a barbecue cook-off, and candlelit tours of Bluff Hall and Gaineswood.

Tuscaloosa also hosts a **Christmas Afloat** celebration. People decorate their boats with colored lights and parade down the Black Warrior River.

Warrior hosts **Christmas on the River** with a boat parade that begins at King's Point Marina and travels up the Warrior River. Santa distributes stockings filled with goodies.

Wetumpka sponsors **Christmas on the Coosa** with a colorfully lighted, themed-float boat parade that passes spectators along the banks of the Coosa River.

Tallassee's water parade has decorated and lighted floats depicting scenes of the Christmas season.

Enjoy a hefty dose of holiday spirit during **Christmas at Arlington** in **Birmingham**. The two-day event is held the first weekend in December at Arlington, a city-owned antebellum home.

Montgomery's Christmas includes **December in Old Alabama Town,** where a nineteenth-century Christmas celebration features music, role playing, demonstrations, and children's activities. During the city's **Cottage Hill District Candlelight Christmas Tour,** several Victorian homes open in Montgomery's oldest residential neighborhood, with candles lining the tour path.

Lowndesboro's Holiday Tour includes open houses, some of which were built before the Civil War. Several area churches also are open.

Tuskegee sponsors a Christmas parade with floats, bands, and drill teams.

Union Springs, a turn-of-the-century town, celebrates the holidays with a parade filled with floats and St. Nick.

Greensboro hosts an open house at **Magnolia Grove.**

Photograph courtesy of Mobile Convention and Visitors Bureau

A Candlelight Christmas is an annual event at Oakleigh in Mobile.

SOUTH ALABAMA

Gulf Shores hosts the **Christmas on the Canal Lighted Boat Parade.**

In **Ariton,** citizen Max Hughes began something simple as a gift to his grandchildren, and his holiday spectacle has since become a town tradition. This 2-mile outdoor display north of Ozark, called **Christmas City,** includes crafts, candy, street entertainers, a stage area, rocking chairs, rides, a Ferris wheel, and a carousel. The spectacle's grand finale is a manger scene.

While in the state's Wiregrass region, don't miss **Christmas at Landmark Park.** Here you'll find samples of turn-of-the-century desserts, hot chocolate, and handmade decorations.

Fort Gaines on **Dauphin Island** relives Christmas much as it was in 1861 when Confederate soldiers camped there.

Mobile offers **Candlelight Christmas** at **Oakleigh,** an 1833 mansion filled for two nights with hundreds of candles. Reenacting a custom dating to Christmas, 1855, local boys dressed as the Mobile Rifle Company pay their respects to a girl dressed as Miss Daisy, the young daughter of the home's former owner, General T. K. Irwin.

Opp's **Christmas Walkway** takes visitors through lighted scenes presented by local churches, civic clubs, and businesses.

Downtown **Fairhope** provides the setting for a **Lighted Night Christmas Parade.**

Foley hosts **Christmas Downtown,** a family event with Christmas music, lighting of Christmas lights, and a parade with floats, bands, clowns, scouts, and Santa.

Daphne hosts a Christmas open house, parade, tree lighting, afternoon parade, lighting of the tree at city hall, and refreshments.

In **Elba Courthouse Square,** Santa and his reindeer join a parade while arts-and-crafts booths offer a variety of gift items.

Hartford's Christmas parade includes Santa, a concert, a live nativity scene, and tree lighting.

In **Monroeville,** holiday traditions include Santa riding his sleigh through downtown streets in a parade that includes floats and marching bands.

For specific dates, admission charges, and information about Christmas events in Alabama, contact the Alabama Bureau of Tourism and Travel at 800/ALABAMA (252-2262).

FESTIVALS

WACKY WEEKEND FUNFESTS

You have to hand it to Alabama—the people here know how to have a good time. When the obvious reasons to celebrate wane, residents are more than willing to conjure up new excuses. Apparently there are no rules about festivals. If you like an idea, then set a date, call your friends, dub it the first annual event, and make history.

There are, of course, the routine festivals—events that pay homage to foods, crafts, music, and the seasons. But Alabama, like most other states, also has its wacky festivals.

The **Rattlesnake Rodeo** is what put the tiny town of Opp on the map. This spring festival includes an arts-and-crafts show and features the world's only rattlesnake race. (Yes, some of the craft items are made from rattlesnake skins.) There also are buck-dancing contests and programs on rattlesnake education and safety.

In the spring Athens hosts another festival called **Homespun** that features demonstrations of Early-American folk art such as basket-weaving, chair-caning, quilting, pottery-making, blacksmithing, and tatting. Guests can observe an antique gristmill in operation and purchase food and home-baked goods.

On May's second Friday and Saturday the city of Arab, near Huntsville, hosts a **Poke Salat Festival.** Known as the poor man's greens, the large and leafy purple-stalked poke plant grows wild, which means that even the poorest will find food, given a liking for the dish. This event includes a cooking contest, street dance, and samples of several poke-salat (salad) dishes.

Gulf Shores hosts the **Blessing of the Fleet** during the last weekend of June. This event originates in a Catholic church tradition of protecting shrimpers and fishing fleets. Crews paint their boats and dress them in brightly colored pennants, flags, and other decorations.

Also on the coast, a **Deep Sea Fishing Rodeo** on Dauphin Island has taken place the third weekend in July since 1929. More than 2,500 saltwater fishermen set out for trophy-size fish. This event kicks off with a Liars' Contest and while crews are at sea those on land can take in the arts and crafts, food, and entertainment.

In mid-August Lookout Mountain Parkway, a long stretch of highway through northeast Alabama, becomes part of a **450-Mile Outdoor Sale,** where shoppers can find everything from canned goods to junk and collectibles.

Russellville hosts a mid-August **Watermelon Festival** that features artists, a car show, the Miss Watermelon beauty pageant, a horse show, live entertainment, a melon-eating contest, games, and of course a seed-spitting contest.

The town of Winfield makes mules king for a day each September. **Mule Day** includes a parade of mules pulling buggies. It also features saddle horses, mule judging, antique cars, arts and crafts, a flea market, the Mule Day Run, a marching-band festival, music, and clogging.

At the **September Catfish Festival** in Greensboro, catfish farmers and locals salute freshwater catfish farming with races, arts and crafts, trade day, entertainment, an antique-car show, and a rodeo. On Saturday visitors may tour the farms by bus. Plan to eat lots of fried catfish and to take home some fillets.

October's first full weekend brings the annual **Tennessee Valley Old Time Fiddlers Convention,** held on the campus of Athens State College in Athens. The event is the flagship of Southern fiddlers' conventions and has been a catalyst for the revival of interest in authentic, old-time music. During the festival the campus overflows with crafts, paintings, and buck dancers.

Loachapoka, near Auburn, hosts a **Syrup Soppin' Festival** each October. Locals demonstrate the process of converting sugarcane into syrup, from cane-crushing in a mule-drawn press to syrup sampling on homemade biscuits—the latter so large that they sometimes are called cat-head biscuits. Sponsored by the Lee County Historical Society, this event proves that traditional syrup sopping is not accomplished with a knife and fork. For some it's as simple as poking a hole in the biscuit and filling it with syrup.

Also in October, Selma hosts a **Tale Tellin' Festival** that draws storytelling giants from across the country. No one, however, is more revered than Alabama's own Kathryn Tucker Windham, a woman in her seventies who claims to live with a ghost named Jeffrey and who has made a career out of telling ghost stories and other tales. This former newspaper woman, who catapulted her writing days into storytelling opportunities, has won the hearts of generations of schoolchildren.

Shrimp is not all you'll find at Gulf Shores's annual Shrimp Festival.

Downtown streets are blocked off for the festival, which also includes crafts and foods.

Blount County hosts a **Covered Bridge Festival** each October in Oneonta. The event celebrates the area's history with a bridge run, bicycle tours, a quilt show, gospel singing, and arts and crafts. There are also demonstrations of candle-making, basket-weaving, milking, sheep-shearing, and a horse show. Fall color tours begin the weekend of the festival and continue through November.

Unique to the Southeast is the mid-November **Southern Wildlife Festival**, which brings together hundreds of artists from across the nation. Artists come to Decatur to exhibit and sell their original paintings, carvings, photographs, books, and merchandise that depict wildlife in natural settings.

As though these aren't wacky enough, here's a look at several other state festivals that will make you want to shout, "Say, what?"

- Elberta holds a **German Sausage Festival** in March and October.
- Headland has a **Daylily Festival** in May.
- Brewton hosts a **Blueberry Festival** each June.
- Robertsdale in central Baldwin County holds a **Honey Bee Festival** in early October.
- Alabama's Gulf Coast holds a **Shrimp Festival** in October.
- Clio is the setting for an October **Chitlin's Festival.**
- Dothan honors peanuts with an annual *November Peanut Festival.*

For details on these and other state festivals, call the Alabama Bureau of Tourism and Travel, 800/ALABAMA (252-2262).

2 NATIVE AMERICANS
POWWOWS AND FESTIVALS

My husband's grandmother declares that her grandmother was full-blooded Cherokee. No one in our family has proven that lineage, but it's quite likely because Native Americans have maintained a strong presence in Alabama.

My children especially like to believe that these memories are sound, and that through their veins may flow the blood of those brave, proud people who settled early on in Alabama. Sometimes I stare at my children and search for signs of that heritage. One of my daughters does have rather olive skin and narrow eyes. Other than that, though, I haven't managed to discover any hint of such ancestry.

Alabama evidences the rich heritage and history of Native Americans throughout the state—in the faces of some of its people, on reservations where tribes continue to live, and at historic sites where their heritage is preserved.

In earlier years the Choctaw were known for their farming in the state's southwest segment, the Cherokee were strong in the northeast section of Alabama, and the Chickasaw roamed the woods of the northwest region. Traces of those early residents remain in a state where native names abound—Tallahatta Springs, Tallassee, Atmore, Bear Creek, and Attalla, for example.

One river was named for the sixteenth-century Choctaw warrior chief Taskalusa. "Taska," meaning "warrior," and "lusa," interpreted as "black," formed the name for the Black Warrior River, which flows through the region early settlers named for Chief Tuscaloosa.

Sequoyah, who invented the Cherokee alphabet, lived in Alabama as a child and later returned during the time he was developing and completing the alphabet. **Sequoyah Caverns** in northeast Alabama is a tribute to this great Cherokee. This attraction is a compact series of chambers with small pools of flowing mineral water that reflect the natural formations.

In 1830, President Andrew Jackson ordered the removal of all tribes living east of the Mississippi River. Many of those forced to leave died along the way during the march the Cherokees called the "Trail of Tears."

Many loved their homeland so much that they hid in mountains, rivers, and swamps to avoid exile. Some south Alabama Native Americans who had fought with Jackson were exempt from leaving.

Alabama has seven recognized tribes, one of which holds federal recognition. Today descendants of those who remained work diligently to preserve their heritage by hosting annual festivals and powwows.

In springtime you can attend Native American festivals at: **DeSoto Caverns** in Childersburg, **Russell Cave National Monument** in Bridgeport, **Wind Creek State Park** in Alexander City, **Tannehill Ironworks Historical State Park** near Birmingham, and in **Moulton** in north Alabama.

In June, **Mount Vernon,** north of Mobile, hosts a **Choctaw Powwow.**

In late summer the Cherokee hold an **August Powwow** and **Green Corn Festival** in Gadsden. The following month **Moundville Archaeological Park,** near Tuscaloosa, hosts a **Native American Festival.**

Huntsville is the site of an **Indian Heritage Festival** in October, and in November the Poarch Creek Indians hold a **Thanksgiving Day Powwow** on their reservation at Atmore. (The **Poarch Creek reservation,** 55 miles north of Mobile, is the setting for **The Bingo Palace,** which each weekend draws hundreds lured by high-stakes games. If you get close, you won't overlook this attraction—from I-65 you will readily see the huge sign declaring "Indian Bingo.")

For details about the state's Native American festivals and events call the Alabama Bureau of Tourism and Travel at 800/ALABAMA (252-2262). For information about Indian Bingo at Atmore, call 334/368-8007.

Photograph courtesy of Alabama Bureau of Tourism and Travel

Throughout the year, Native Americans host festivals and powwows paying tribute to their heritage.

3 PILGRIMAGES
JOURNEYS INTO YESTERDAY

Alabama's roots are unearthed and showcased almost year-round during pilgrimages into some of the state's most majestic homes. From north to south throughout the state, many residents each year set aside time to share with visitors their personal worlds and their heritage. Such pilgrimages include tours not only of homes, but also of churches, and, as is the case in Selma, a candlelight cemetery tour.

These guided walks give the curious a chance to look behind the white columns, double doors, and azalea-framed structures that hold enormous allure.

Tours are often led by a home's occupant who can point out scars, nooks, and crannies that detail the structure's history written between its thick walls. Often restored to its original appearance, a home paints a picture of the region, its history, its struggles, and its growth.

Afternoon tea and delicacies are served in many homes during these pilgrimages.

Springtime pilgrimages take place in Athens, Cullman, Eufaula, Huntsville, Mobile, Mooresville, Selma, Talladega, Tuscaloosa, and Union Springs.

Montgomery hosts a pilgrimage tour in June, and Camden polishes its silver for a September open house. Demopolis and Eutaw hold their pilgrimages each October, while Lowndesboro and Opelika hold December pilgrimages.

Photograph by Milton Fullman

Just west of downtown Eufaula, Kendall Manor Inn has become a bed and breakfast where visitors feel they have stepped back in time.

You can use a pilgrimage as an excuse to visit a town or region. While you are there, take time to explore other area attractions such as museums, lakes, botanical gardens, and old churches.

There is a charge for visiting homes open for pilgrimages. In most cases you can purchase a ticket at the door of a pilgrimage home or at a central location. You may get a discount if you buy a multihouse admission ticket.

For a calendar of Alabama events, with dates and times of pilgrimages, call the Alabama Bureau of Tourism and Travel at 800/ALABAMA (252-2262).

3 BARBECUE IN DIXIE

SOUTHERN BORN AND HICKORY SMOKED

Years ago a sportscaster, who was visiting Tuscaloosa to broadcast an Alabama gridiron clash on national television, whiled away a lull by talking about the barbecued ribs he had discovered in T-Town at a place called **Dreamland.** Some credit those on-air comments for lifting Dreamland to nationwide attention. Dreamland, which has since expanded to Birmingham and Mobile, is far from plush, but the barbecue is worth the trip.

The secret, so they say, of barbecue-smoked foods in the South is the hickory. Then there are the sauces—as different as the people who make them. Some barbecue kings brew a thick sauce; others make theirs with a vinegar base. Some like it hot; some like it mild. Some like it thick; some thin.

It doesn't much matter to barbecue lovers, who find in Alabama some of the world's best barbecue. It isn't unusual for those who have lived or visited here to order barbecue shipped to far-off places. Each package of barbecue delivers a piece of Dixie, succulent and inviting.

Ribs are the specialty at the world-renowned Dreamland Barbecue.

Barbecue restaurants are scattered throughout the state, and most are worth trying. Although pork is most popular, cooked over slow hickory embers, chicken and beef are also barbecued. Typically the meats are served with a choice of fried potatoes, coleslaw, and baked beans, with a tall glass of iced tea to round out the meal. (Be prepared to tell your server if you want your tea sweetened or unsweetened—most restaurants offer the option.)

A barbecue weekend is a good way to get to know Alabama firsthand, and you can do so from just about any starting point.

A barbecue breakfast is an option at several places, including **The Golden Rule** in Irondale, east of Birmingham. Michael Matsos owns the restaurant, which dates to 1892 when only a dirt road passed by out front.

Bob Sykes Bar-B-Q, west of Birmingham in Bessemer, also serves breakfast.

Ollie's Barbecue, a Birmingham tradition since 1926, is operated by a fourth generation of the McClung family. A guest book in the restaurant, which is near the campus of the University of Alabama at Birmingham, verifies that diners come here from all over the globe. Save room for the homemade pies!

Hosie's Bar-B-Que, near the **Jazz Hall of Fame** in downtown Birmingham, specializes in ribs, but you also will find fried green tomatoes, fried okra, pigs' ears, and banana pudding here.

Another memorable barbecue spot is **Greenbrier Restaurant** where, years ago, country-music stars would sit atop the building and sing to lure crowds. These days, the barbecue alone is enough to draw hungry diners down two-lane Old Alabama Highway 20 not far from Huntsville. You might also sample the catfish and seafood.

For many years **Dobbs' Bar-B-Que** has been the place in Dothan for barbecue. As a young man barely out of his teens in 1910, Evell Dobbs plunged into the business with a venture in Tallassee. He moved his restaurant to Dothan in 1948. Like most barbecue businesses, this one's not fancy, but it lures travelers and locals alike with its juicy meats and tomato-based sauce. The strawberry cake is also excellent. And there's no waiting for iced tea refills—the server leaves a pitcher right on your table.

In the 1920s the hickory aroma of **Big Bob Gibson's backyard barbecue** became a Decatur enticement that led to his opening a restaurant. Today the eatery bearing his name still does business, and the demand is so intense that the drive-through window opens daily at 7 a.m. The restaurant is now overseen by Gibson's grandson, Don McLemore, who grew up hopping cars and splitting chickens under his granddad's watchful eye. Don't miss the barbecue turkey and chicken served with a trademarked white sauce that is bottled and sold in grocery stores under the Big Bob Gibson name.

Betty's Bar-B-Q is a favorite among Anniston locals, who sometimes opt for side orders of butter beans and cornbread. (Time the daily special just right, and you can order chicken and dressing or homemade spaghetti.) A sign posted here reflects the atmosphere: "There are no strangers at Betty's . . . only friends we haven't met."

For more about the best barbecue places in a town, contact the chamber of commerce or just stop and ask one of the locals.